HOW TO HAVE PASSIVE INCOME

Book Description:

Is it accurate to say that you are prepared to put your cash into making automated revenue streams that blow up your month to month pay? These are probably the most sweltering, demonstrated strategies that you can begin with, today.

You 're not going to get rich procuring a compensation. You really want to take those investment funds and bring in cash from cash. But how? It can be harrowing and risky to invest in new income streams for the first time. The possibility that you will lose cash is high. That is the reason you really want an aide very much like this one.

In Passive Income Ideas for 2019, I detail probably the most worthwhile strategies for acquiring extra pay accessible for the cutting edge financial backer. I take a genuine, unfiltered check out promising circumstances in web-based media, outsourcing, associate showcasing and leasing. There is genuine cash to be made here!

In this thoughts guide you'll learn:

- Why passive income will get you where you want to

go How drop-shipping works and how to get started selling

- What affiliate marketing is and how to make money this way

How to invest as someone interested in passive income

.

How to leverage social media for passive income generation

.

About renting, website flipping, selling eBooks and being a creative

Anything is possible when you 're presently not a captive to your regularly scheduled check. You'll lose a few. Furthermore you'll win some as well. Sooner or later, you'll simply continue to win. That is the point at which your life changes.

Discover how to genuinely make automated revenue streams that will liberate you from your present place of employment. It's simpler than you might suspect, and everything necessary is responsibility and a sharp mind!

Learn how to begin with automated revenue in this aide.
Purchase the aide, and start earning!

Introduction

Are you struggling to make money? Do you feel like you are spending most of your time, yet you have nothing to show for it? Do you admire those millionaires and billionaires on TV and wonder how they do it? If the answer is yes, then you might want to ask yourself how you can get out of your own way and start making more money. The appropriate response is to that is additionally straightforward; you are not doing all that you can to get more cash-flow. You might consider how that is assuming you are burning through the entirety of your waking hours working. The appropriate response is you don't have a PASSIVE INCOME stream. For quite a long time, rich individuals have perceived that it's not how much work you do that makes you rich, that it is the nature of work that you do. You can go the entire day trying sincerely yet at the same time get compensated least wages for it. There is additionally the risk of getting terminated unexpectedly which causes you to lose everything assuming you were not prepared.

Rich individuals comprehend that the cash They have should work for them. They put their cash in roads that get them more cash-flow. They, notwithstanding, don't plunk down and partake in their riches. They continue to place their cash in roads that continue to create a gain. They ensure that they make money even when they are not involved in said investments. This is which isolates the rich and the poor.

If you have a little money and a lot of patience, then this is the book for you. Dynamic pay is the cash you get in your financial balance that you procure from a task you do. It is the thing that the vast majority depend on to make due. For a really long time, individuals have been encouraged to set aside cash before they use the remainder. Regardless of whether your bills take up a tremendous level of your income, you can in any case save something. If you can't save anything, then that tells you that you are living beyond your means.

Don 't place all of your cash in a bank and accept that it is protected there. It very well may be protected, however it isn't effectively shield your future. That cash is the thing that you should take out and put resources into easy revenue creating adventures. Passive income is that which you earn even when you are not working for it. You get cash from doing nothing essentially. To procure an automated revenue, the greater part of the work is done forthright, and afterward the return will stream in however long the speculation stays dynamic. The cash you get month to month may not be huge, however in case you save it for quite a while, along with build revenue, you will see the distinction. You must show restraint before you see some unmistakable effect of your effect, yet when it begins, it never stops.

There are numerous ways of making automated revenue and the profits from each differ. The more the return, the more you might need to reach out. I'm not saying you need to invest all your energy on it. I'm saying you must be involved. You might have to invest a little effort to cause the speculation to procure more, yet it can in any case run without it. In case you disdain taking care of business, this isn't really for you. This is on the grounds that easy revenue isn't a pyramid scheme. The work might be requesting, however the outcomes make it all worthwhile.

The way that easy revenue is a certain method of bringing in additional cash doesn't imply that the field stays inflexible. You will continually need to realize what is changing in the business could improve things greatly in your profits over the long haul. Check out patterns and what individuals are searching for, yet you actually need to add our character to it to make it even better.

Why the Need for Passive Income?

Even however we continue to say that automated revenue is cash we don 't need to work for, we need to recall that we exchanged that cash for time at some point previously. Automated revenue is an immediate season of consistent endeavors throughout some time. Regardless of whether you actually acquire from something you made ten years prior, there is no disgrace in advising that to individuals. There would not be anything exploitative here particularly assuming you accomplished some work that is taking care of years later.

You will be free to pursue other things instead of chasing after money. You may still have your active income, but your days will be freer for you to rest and spend time with family instead of taking a second job to meet your basic requirements. Some people earn a lot of passive income that they can leave jobs they hate to pursue what they are passionate about. They are sorted even if their passions don't pay them right away.

.

You will be able to plan for the future with the extra money. The greatest fear among working people is what will happen if they retired, and they are more worried if they are unable to put something aside for retirement when they can no longer work. Passive income eliminates that from your mind because as you work for your day to day expenses, your investments are working for your retirement.

.

If you are trying to build multiple passive income streams, you can do so as opposed to traditional jobs here you are limited to a desk in a particular place. The internet becomes your workplace as you can communicate with clients and potential customers without leaving your home.

.

With passive income, there is nowhere else to go but up if you play your cards right. This doesn't include risky investments. It includes the streams of passive income that have worked for many years. Even if the return starts out small, there is steady growth over a period of time as long as people are still interested in what you are selling. This will also happen if you keep marketing yourself and establishing yourself as an authority on a certain subject matter.

.

Passive income is the foundation for wealth in the long run. The discipline it takes to work on something other than the one you have to do makes you appreciate the money you make. You may be a business owner that makes a lot of money. Until you make your money work for you aka investing, you are still not wealthy.

Passive income saves you the most precious commodity that you can't gain back once lost–time. If you can exchange the time, you spend chasing money to pay bills and survive then you have won in life. As John Wooden so elegantly stated, "Don't let making a living prevent you from making alife."

This book accompanies a FREE Bonus section area as a gift. You can download them free of charge. The free substance can be found at the lower part of this book.

Chapter 1: Dropshipping

The best an ideal opportunity to establish a tree was 20 years prior. The second-best an ideal opportunity to establish a tree is today.
Chinese Proverb

Drop delivering has as of late acquired footing in the automated revenue space. It has particularly been truly productive due to individuals' adoration for web based shopping. Here, you as the merchant have a site, yet you don't really claim the item you are selling. It resembles a financier between the client and an outsider dealer. You never see the item on the grounds that the item is straightforwardly sent from the outsider vender to the customer. The outsider here is a distributer or a maker. You as a drop transporter never handle the stock, along these lines, lessening the requirement for an actual area as with regular retailers.

How Does Drop Shipping Work?

The primary thing to see is that Drop delivering is a help that is given to a client by an individual behind a PC. The producer produces things available to be purchased yet doesn't sell straightforwardly to the last purchaser. This is on the grounds that it seldom seems OK to sell a thing at a time if they manage a large number of items at a go. They offer their items at a lower cost in mass and have practically zero buy necessities, making it advantageous for retailers with a great deal of capital and wholesalers to purchase straightforwardly from them. The distributer purchases from the producer and afterward raise the expense somewhat higher to create a gain. They likewise sell the majority of their items in mass instead of a solitary thing. The end purchaser, in this way, can buy things whatever the number from a retailer. The retailer purchases from a distributer and raises the expense considerably higher to take into account their net revenues. These are the three gatherings of individuals that are accessible in an inventory network, and in this way as a drop transporter, you are a retailer. The outsourcing model isn't apparent to the end purchaser by any stretch of the imagination. You as the drop transporter can buy your items from any of the three gatherings regardless of whether you are a retailer. However long any of them will send their items to your end client, they are"outsourcing" for you.
Step 1: Order Placement by Customer

A client surfs through your specialty site and observes an item that they need to purchase. You as the vendor receives a message illuminating you regarding the buy. All the while, the client gets an affirmation message of the buy. The request is consequently produced by the product and emailed to the two players. The installment is likewise naturally handled by an installment programming, and affirmations are made to both parties.

Step 2: Order situation to the supplier

The request affirmation message is shipped off the provider with the goal that they can process and transport the request to the client. The provider charges the absolute expense of the thing from the vendor's record. Their cost will be lower than what is charged by the vendor. The cost will incorporate request handling charges, delivering expenses and the expense of the thing. It is consequently dependent upon the dealer to have considered this when they charged the consumer.

Step 3: Order Dispatch from the provider warehouse

The provider boxes and ships the thing to client contingent upon how quick their administration is. This ought to be incorporated when advertising to the client. The vendor's logo, address, and contact number are what will show up on the case and not that of the provider. After delivery, an alarm is shipped off the vendor alongside a following number for the request. They additionally send a receipt for bookkeeping purposes to the merchant.

Step 4: The vendor illuminates the client about the shipment
 An email alert is shipped off the client with the request following data by the dealer through the store's product. The request is finished at this point.

How to Find Suppliers to Work with

As I said previously, the distinction among progress and disappointment in outsourcing is a solid provider. The end client doesn't realize that there is an outsider associated with the deal. Thusly you will be the one answerable assuming that the thing isn't transported, is harmed or of low quality. Subsequently, one requirements to work with a provider that will function admirably with your plan of action. You will likewise have to separate between real wholesalers from pretenders and tricksters. How might you separate the phony from the genuine wholesalers you may
ask?
They want you to pay them a monthly fee instead of charging you for the items you order from them. A legitimate supplier may charge a processing fee, but it is a reasonable amount, and they explain what they are charging you for so you know beforehand. Legitimate fees you will encounter are order processing fees that are added to each order you make. They will also have a minimum amount of goods you buy as your first purchase to weed out buyers from window shoppers. Instead of buying the items, you can advance them the total amount for an order that will go into your merchant account.

If they are claiming to be wholesalers and yet they are selling directly to customers. This makes the prices go way up as they want to make as much money as they do if they sell directly to the client. That will eat into your profit margins.

There are numerous manners by which a shipper can track down discount providers to work with.
1. Getting in contact with manufacturers

If you know the items you need to offer, searching for makers to work with isn't hard. You should simply determining from them a rundown of their wholesalers. From that point you can search for the one that drops transporting and requests prerequisites to set up a record with them.

2. Make utilization of the internet

The web is brimming with data as everybody is publicizing on the web. Contingent upon your specialty, many individuals offer the help you really want. Be cautious as you can likewise experience con artists. Don't simply make due with the main providers that you see on the top page. Go further into the web search tools as numerous great wholesalers might be concealed in the outcome look. View at the proposals instead of the plan of their sites. Try not to abandon the main attempt and don't anticipate getting a decent distributer immediately.

3. Scout, your rival's supplier

Finding a distributer is difficult and what preferable method for getting one over great old
 style undercover work. You can arrange from your rival. You can call the number on the return address which is bound to be the supplier. 4. Trade fairs and shows

Many producers go to exchange fairs where they network with possible retailers. The exchange fairs are organized by the items, and you can without much of a stretch pinpoint makers in your specialty. Some are free, and others have a participation charge. Exploit numerous makers in the equivalent place.

5. Directories

There are numerous registries in the market that you can search for providers in your specialty. They incorporate SaleHoo, Doba, Wholesale Central thus on.

Attributes of a Good Supplier

.Professionalism and experience

If you are new at outsourcing, an expert agent will actually want to talk you through the interaction and guarantee you en route. They can likewise have the option to respond to your inquiries on any theme you may have.

.Around the clock support
 Suppliers that answer the customer's inquiries quickly motivate certainty with the client.
 Tech-savvy organization

Because outsourcing is done from all edges of the globe, innovation is the main thing that is bringing together every player in the game. Orders and installments must be done quickly and safely through best in class programming to further develop client experience. At the absolute minimum, they ought to have email connectivity.

.Good location

If you are a drop transporter, you might need to search for a provider that is near practically the entirety of your customers to further develop the conveyance time while decreasing delivery costs.

.Efficiency
 A decent provider thinks often about your consumer loyalty which will promise you a recurrent client. They will give great quality items and handle the transportation cycle with care and urgency.

How to Pick the Right Product for Dropshipping

Drop delivering is a web-based business, and the most ideal way to realize what individuals need is to look on the Internet. With SEO, it is straightforward what individuals are hoping to purchase online through catchphrase look. You can likewise see what individuals in your geographic area, what to purchase and afterward the thing is in during a specific season. Recall that outsourcing is certifiably not a static business and those that develop make the most money.

Consider the cost at which the provider is advertising. The cost at which you offer the client ought to be sensible; any other way, you should offer telephone support for affirmation. The suggested value range for most webbased clients is $50-$200. Sell an item with a MAP (least publicized value) estimating so that there isn't a lot of distinction in costs among you and the competition.

Look at the versatility and life span of your business. Your item ought to have the option to endure for an extremely long period and the tides of patterns. Consider how you can advertise the item to expected clients. Sell things that go together so the client doesn't click away from your site. Sell things that don't change with time or transitory goods.

Look at what clients need to track down the ideal things to sell. If something can be bought at a local store, then it is not worth the time. Keep away from greater and delicate items as they are costly to transport and may separate during transportation. Likewise, keep away from things that could be defective when the client tests it out. You need to maintain a business without returns and objections to continue getting positive reviews.

Advantages of Dropshipping

1. Starting capital is little contrasted with having a physical location All a shipper requires is a site to show the items they are selling. They don't have to purchase any stock or extra room to keep it. This diminishes the beginning money to an absolute minimum. The Dropshipping model ensures that you make a sale first before buying it from the supplier and even then, the burden of packaging and shipping lies with the third party. The expense of maintaining the business is likewise low as there is no actual store to run. Overhead costs like lease, representatives' compensations, office supplies, and licenses are not something a drop transporter needs to stress over. They just need a PC, dependable web association and a site to do their business which is month to month benefits and can be gotten to at a low cost

2. It is a simple business to start

Compared to numerous organizations today, beginning a Drop delivering business can be simple. All that you want to be familiar with maintaining a web-based business can be gotten to on the web. You can likewise continue further developing your promoting ability subsequent to beginning the business as there isn't anything for you to lose. Contrasted with financial specialists with a stock, you don't have to stress over stock taking, office the board. As you won't deal with any stock, the pressure of supplanting completed items, pressing and transportation orders to customers or getting a distribution center isn't yours. Ensuring orders get to the customers and managing returns is additionally another person's business.

3. You are not bound to any location
 You can begin a Drop delivering business anyplace on the planet as long as

you have a PC and a solid web association. With the accessibility of enormous online business stores that can assist you with interfacing with producers straightforwardly, you can work with anybody on the planet today. Installments can likewise be made online without the shipper, client and the maker truly meeting eye to eye. All you really want is trust and dependability combined with availability to the internet.

 4. You can sell a wide scope of items

A standard retailer stresses over space and cost of buying stock when concluding what they need to sell. This isn't true with drop transporters. They should simply check in the event that the customer has the item in stock and afterward they put it up on the site available to be purchased. A drop transporter can have different
 classes and choices for various clients as long as the outsider can supply it to the customer.

 5. It requires some investment for the new business to scale upward

The issue standard retail model is that with more clients, the handling of requests increments and in this way the need to enlist more stuff. This weight is missing for this situation as, notwithstanding the increment in orders, it's the provider that arrangements with bundling and transportation. This doesn't influence the shipper in any capacity aside from possibly making installments all the more oftentimes which scarcely appears to be a con. The other work that might increment perhaps in client care yet that can be tackled with one worker or two.

Disadvantages of Dropshipping

1. Some specialties have low-benefit margins
 Depending on the specialty that you decide to go into, there is the chance of

creating a little gain for each thing. First and foremost, the dealer may under-cost to get traffic to the site. The person should sell a great deal of items so they can get more cash-flow over the long haul which can require a significant stretch of time to occur. There is likewise a great deal of rivalry on the web, and the clients will wind up picking the site that offers the most minimal price.

2. You need to pick the right supplier

Unless you have the highest level of trust that your provider will convey the items to the clients at the perfect opportunity and in the right condition, your business will undoubtedly fall flat. Standard retailers don't deal with this issue as they can guarantee quality control in their stock and delivery process. You will, in this way, need to analyze until you get the right accomplice. Client objections will most certainly be coordinated towards you in spite of the incident not being our shortcoming. Guarantee you speak with your providers continually to further develop the delivery cycle and lessen complaints.

3. The difficulties of managing numerous suppliers

As a drop transporter, it isn't remarkable to manage numerous providers simultaneously. Some might be reliable, however some may not, and the client might purchase things that come from various providers. To start with, there might be significant
contrasts in transportation costs that may not sound good to the client. Figuring distinctive delivery charges from various providers might be hard on the grounds that the expense might be a lot for a client to deal with. You may, in this manner, need to normalize the charges which might come from your pocket.

Despite being a simple method for making easy revenue, Drop delivering requires a ton of devotion and difficult work. It's anything but an easy money scam. These difficulties can be survived assuming the dealer utilizes various procedures from everybody else.

Chapter 2: Affiliate Marketing

Residual pay is automated revenue that comes in each month whether or not you appear. It's the point at which you presently don't get compensated on your own endeavors alone, yet you get compensated on the endeavors of hundreds or even a great many others and your cash! It's one of the keys to independence from the rat race and time freedom.

-Steve Fisher

Affiliate showcasing is the ideal method for bringing in additional cash. With offshoot promoting, you bring in cash by putting your crowd onto an organization's item, and assuming they wind up getting, you procure a commission. You resemble a center man between a buyer and an organization. You should comprehend the four players in the whole subsidiary showcasing process.

.The product creator or the seller is the person that owns a certain brand and could benefit from people buying their product. .

An affiliate network is a program that links product creators to interests affiliate marketers. Even though the product creator can get affiliate marketers on their own, it is safer for the affiliate marketer to use an affiliate link. They can track their earnings and ensure they are paid on time through a legitimate affiliate network.

.

An affiliate marketer is a person that takes advantage of an offer to market products from a product creator to get people to but their product in exchange for a percentage of the sale. They are in charge of aggressive marketing as they earn from what they sell. A super affiliate is someone who is driving up the sales of the product they promote.

.The end consumer who buys the product promoted by the affiliate marketer.
 In member promoting, you can bring in cash as both an item maker or as a partner marketer.

4 Steps to Become a Product Creator

An item maker can be known by many names. They incorporate vender, shipper, a brand, seller or retailer. As a vender, you make an item and have a partner marker sell it for you.

Step 1: Look for an incredible item thought

As a vender, don't bounce into making an item without thoroughly considering the thought. Think about an item that many individuals need in their life and takes care of a specific issue they have. Set aside effort to consummate the plan to concoct an item individuals will purchase. Investigate items in well known specialties that individuals are looking for on the web. Rather than concocting a thought from flimsy air, think about seeing what as of now exists on the lookout and enhance it. Try not to be inflexible with regards to thoughts; adjust your perspective relying upon what you find out with regards to a specific specialty. It is in every case better to search for motivation from things that you are as of now inspired by or learned about. This saves you time as you probably are aware the significant essentials that you should fabricate upon.

Step 2: Research to check whether individuals like the thought and assuming there is a need it fills

After getting the possibility that you need to seek after, do statistical surveying to check whether individuals would purchase. The market is the genuine trial of a fruitful item, and individuals would purchase what they need instead of what you are offering to them. You can utilize accessible exploration instruments like Buzzsumo to realize what individuals are right now into. When you are certain, you can test the market by inquiring as to whether they would purchase the item. Assuming this is the case, let them preorder so you can check whether they would burn through cash on your product.

Step 3: Make the product

There are numerous assets online that tell you precisely how to make incredible computerized items. Regardless of whether its web-based courses and online classes, educational eBooks or webcasts; adhere to directions from individuals who are proficient in each field make a helpful item that takes care of an issue. Make sure to convey the completed item to the purchasers that pre-requested and get some criticism on it. Make a site that permits individuals to study your item and purchase it.

Step 4: Join an offshoot organization or search for partner advertisers to showcase your product
 It's at last an ideal opportunity to acquire members ready. You can join a partner arrange and interface with members. One thing you need to remember is that
 the most valuable partners are the ones currently in your specialty. They as of now have a crowd of people that needs to purchase items like yours, and this can convert into deals for your item. So how might you get offshoot advertisers in your specialty? Search online for spring up locales that are in a similar specialty as you and pitch to them a collaboration.

Something worth being thankful for to recollect is that assuming your item dives deep in a specific specialty, the more straightforward it will be to get individual shippers to help you. A proposition on a forthcoming organization should detail how both of you will benefit over the long haul. For you get individuals who will showcase your item, you need to give them a decent arrangement on the commission. If you offer commissions between 45-60%, then more people will be willing to come on board. The explanation large organizations offer low commissions is that they have many member advertisers and their item is not difficult to showcase as individuals definitely know the item. Since your item is new, you won't get a similar outcome in the event that you are parsimonious with pay-outs. They are considerably bound to work more diligently to acquire clients as they are persuaded. Search for YouTube directs in a similar specialty and inform them regarding your item and make them an offer.

If you have a site as of now, begin composing blog entries educating individuals concerning your item and notice that you would likewise like partner advertisers to come ready. Growing an email rundown and sharing on your online media stages can likewise draw in some offshoot marketers.

4 Ways to Make Money as an Affiliate Marketer

1. Join an Affiliate network

Joining a member program empowers you to see items that are on special and need partner advertising. At the point when you pick a subsidiary program, for instance, Amazon Associates, you can get a sharable member connect that you can impart to your crowd that they can snap to purchase. That is the connection that recognizes you and is the one you will use in the entirety of your promoting strategies.

2. Review items online

People lie to see what they are purchasing and what preferred method for doing that over watching somebody testing it for them. By showing individuals how great the item is, you will catch their consideration to such an extent that when you give them a source of inspiration to purchase the item, they will do precisely that. Guarantee you give genuine audits and sell just items you make certain about. That is the main way you will end up being an expert in your specialty. I think at this point you realize you need to pick a specialty and stick to it. You can compose your audit on a site or make a video survey and post on YouTube. A sharp method for getting more cash is to do numerous surveys in one and put all the member joins in the post for individuals to pick what they like best. On your site, you can have connections to items you have attempted, tried and adored. They can be items, assets or different things you feel certain about.

3. Comparing products

This is a decent method for getting individuals to purchase utilizing your connection as there are numerous comparative items that individuals think that it is difficult to browse. In case an individual coincidentally finds your post, they will undoubtedly purchase since they were looking for the best of the a few items. The examination brings to the table top to bottom knowledge into the two items and consider giving them a legit recommendation.

4. E-mail marketing

This is a famous promoting methodology that has procured some offshoot advertisers 6 figure commissions. For any subsidiary advertiser, a local area of individuals that regard and trust your perspective is indispensable as they are probably going to be your clients when you propose an item. The greater your email list the more influence you have when you have an item to advance. But how can you build an email list that you can convert into a loyal customer base? First, you will need software that creates for you a landing page and an automated response email marketing tool.

Remember that individuals will prefer your email list assuming you offer them something that they need. It shouldn't generally be tied in with offering something to them yet rather like them by giving them lead magnets. A lead magnet is a device utilized by offshoot advertisers to draw in individuals to pursue organizers and planning imagine that individuals would need so they continue to pay special mind to a greater amount of it. A decent lead magnet is free, easy to see, directly an email list. They incorporate free courses, devices, eBooks essentially anything you can forthright, identified with the site specialty and in particular it ought to offer some benefit to the client. At the point when you make a lead magnet, get its uncommon URL and transfer it to an available site. A tip here is to shrewdly add your offshoot joins in your lead magnet to expand profits.

Remember we discussed presentation pages before, yet it has different names as well. It is additionally called a catch, crush or lead page. Its fundamental point is to draw in the guest and make him, or she join with their email. Whatever the software or design you use, you then connect the landing page with your email collecting tool.

Automation is the substance of easy revenue and in subsidiary advertising specifically. You don't should be continually composing and refreshing substance for your email list when you can plan content and still be powerful in different regions. In email showcasing, get an autoresponder that circles back to a progression of messages that increase the value of your supporters and unobtrusively helps them to remember what you are selling. Try not to spam people groups mail as they will without a doubt withdraw. Keep them interested with more free stuff, and use language then makes them feel like your friend and not a customer.

Advantages of Affiliate Marketing

1. Low overhead and modest to start

Whether you choose to turn into an item designer or an offshoot advertiser, you just need a PC, a site or YouTube channel and web association. The main installment you will make concerning facilitating the website.

2. Products are digital

Digital items are modest to make since they don't consume space in a distribution center, and they don't expect delivery to arrive at the buyer. In the event that somebody is a partner advertiser, they don't have to make any item whatsoever, hence, saving themselves some time.

3. It's flexible

Compared to different organizations and occupations, there is no assigned time or spot that one ought to be at to succeed. However long you have a consistent web association and are devoted, you will succeed. There is additionally no restriction to the quantity of subsidiary items you can showcase simultaneously. Automation means that you can earn even when you are offline.

4. Earning potential

As I expressed previously, individuals are making 6-7 figure livelihoods by advancing items on the web. Contingent upon your systems towards procuring an automated revenue, nothing is preventing you from earning enough to pay the bills out of offshoot marketing.

5. It should be possible corresponding to other online businesses.

Many individuals are doing on the web business, and subsidiary promoting can be incorporated into another revenue source. Since all you require is a subsidiary connection that can be put anyplace on a site, it doesn't need to meddle with anything. Email showcasing is mechanized; in this way one can procure without checking in.

Disadvantages of Affiliate Marketing

1. It requires some investment before somebody will bring in cash. For the individuals who believe that associate showcasing is making easy money conspire, they will be frustrated as certain individuals have remained for a year prior to bringing in any cash. It requires persistence and perseverance.

2. As with any lucrative endeavor, certain individuals capture your offshoot, and you don't get your bonus when they utilize your connection. To be protected, you can take a stab at utilizing URL concealing to shield your member joins from cybercriminals.

3. Choosing an awful partner organization can discolor your standing and will prompt question among your reliable adherents. Guarantee you work with brands that have a similar worth as you.

4. You can't dissect the numbers separated from the traffic that is going to the item site, deals, and returns. You won't know whatever else about the client. Accordingly, showcasing will consistently be by some coincidence. You are not a piece of the business module except if you are the item creator.

5. Unless you are in a trustworthy subsidiary organization, you may not be paid for your work, and it is absolutely impossible to find the company.

6. It is a cutthroat space to be in particularly in the event that an organization is offering a high commission. The test is the means by which you can showcase the item while standing apart from the rest.

Mistakes to Avoid as A New Affiliate Marketer

Don't be that individual that is simply hoping to make a speedy buck from individuals. Individuals can generally let know if all you are doing is promoting an item as opposed to acting naturally. Try not to consider yourself a merchant of the item however as an impact of individuals towards an item. You should simply submit an idea with every one of the significant realities and let individuals choose. Assuming you can, try out the items first prior to prescribing them to your dedicated endorsers of stay away from unexpected issues. Try not to adorn or oversell something on the off chance that you don't know how it functions. It is a certain method for losing credibility.

Pick one partner program and ideal that as opposed to joining numerous projects. As a novice, you are as yet inexperienced, and you want to learn and commit errors before you can fill your plate with more work. Gain from others doing likewise on the web and be great at one thing first. You will discover that you can get more cash-flow that way than plunging your toe in everything.

If you are advancing different items, track every single one of them so you can drop whatever isn't procuring you anything. There is no compelling reason to continue pushing something not changing over well in deals. With a decent partner network like Amazon, they offer extraordinary following IDs that can assist you with dealing with all your links.

Avoid changing specialties no matter what. At the point when you have great subscribership, they anticipate something from you, and to that end they are following you. Regardless of whether you presume something is superior to what you are as of now doing, make an alternate site for it as opposed to befuddling your adherents. Own one thing prior to continuing on to something else.

Chapter 3: Passive Income Investments

Compound interest is the eighth marvel of the world. He who comprehends it acquires it ... he who doesn't ... pays it. Accumulate interest is the most impressive power known to mankind. Build interest is the best numerical revelation ever. - Albert Einstein

What Are Passive Income Investments?

Passive income investing is wHere you put up your money in capital investments such as mutual funds, treasury bonds, and bills, fixed accounts and even stocks. You acquire a pay from either procuring a level of the organization you are putting resources into or you bring in profits or premium from the cash you decide to contribute. Here, you are simply financing the contributing and not straightforwardly overseeing it, making it uninvolved. You will acquire leftover pay that is determined by intensifying what you decide to contribute. As a novice, you will just place in your cash once into an automated revenue speculation and from that point forward, you will have normal stores from your investments.

People who are working will more often than not disregard the way that they will not be working for eternity. They need to begin making arrangements for retirement by investigating their pay, their day by day costs and how much cash they can save to keep up with a similar way of life when they resign. Youngsters are infamous for enjoying the high life and failing to remember that this is the best an ideal opportunity to begin saving as they have no genuine commitments. Contributing doesn't have an age limit. A few guardians open up schooling assets for their youngsters when they conceived and save. This diminishes the weight when the opportunity arrives to pay from school. Some show the significance of saving by opening for them their own investment accounts. What they need to do is instruct them that cash can likewise develop all alone whenever set perfectly positioned. These children then grow while learning to invest so that they make more money.

11 Examples of Passive Income Investments

1. Crowdfunded Real Estate
 For some years, we have accepted that turning into a land head honcho requires a ton of cash-flow to get into. A more straightforward method for getting into land is by putting resources into crowdfunded adventures. There are different organizations like Fundraiser that permit you to store as low as $500 and get a stake in somewhere around 48 land projects. There are a few organizations like Rich Uncles that you can enlist with the expectation of complimentary that deal much more reasonable choices. Rich Uncles, for instance, has a deal called Student Housing REIT (Real Estate Investment Trust) that one can contribute just $5. Many organizations are attempting to bring land speculations more standard and are focusing on low-pay earners.

 2. Certificate of Deposit (CDs) Ladders

CDs are an extraordinary way for novices to begin on the grounds that there are no essentials in what one can begin with contrasted with numerous other capital ventures. The way that they are likewise accessible in nearby banks is wonderful as you can open a CD record without any problem. It is generally safe on the grounds that a FDIC guarantees individual CDs for up to $250,000 and shared services for up to $500,000. It's generally simple to pull out your cash from a CD and is an extraordinary method for procuring a pay with least exertion. The more extended the CD like five years or more, the higher the premium the bank presents on it. You can buy CDs in online banks such as CIT bank.

 3. Dividend Income

When you invest in a company by buying the shares or stocks in that company, then you earn a dividend based on the number of shares you have. To glean some significant knowledge about venture, you should follow the tycoon financial backer Warren Buffet as he has a ton of insight to partake in the subject. Profits can be paid quarterly or yearly relying upon the organization being referred to. Prior to putting resources into an organization, take a gander at their set of experiences and master forecasts on their future so you don't wind up putting resources into an organization that will not be around for quite a while. To get more cash-flow, think about contributing for the long stretch. To put resources into stocks, open a speculation account with an authorized stockbroker so your venture is protected. You should pay a little charge to purchase stocks, yet that's it in a nutshell. Continue to investigate great organizations to put resources into as you construct your portfolio.

4. Bonds (Fixed Income)
 Bonds are extraordinary as their financing costs were going up for the beyond couple of years. Regardless of whether the financing costs stay consistent or go up, bonds are a decent method for procuring automated revenue, particularly assuming that you hold them until they mature. They are useful for long haul financial backers who won't pull out the cash before the development time frame is up. There are different bonds to choose from such as an individual corporate bond, the 7-10-year IEF, municipal bonds or the Pimco Total Return Fund which is a fixed income fund.

5. Peer to Peer Lending (P2P)

You can turn into a shylock or something to that affect, i.e., loaning to individuals who need credit yet can't get it from conventional advance organizations. A few organizations that permit you to put resources into their shared loaning business with low costing bonds (as low as $10) and paying out returns going from 3-8%. They have no limitation on when you can have your cash back. You can simply stroll in and pull out any sum you need. It is a dangerous business as certain borrowers won't take care of the cash they get. You will likewise have to put away much more cash to get exorbitant premium rates.

6. Private Equity Investments

Some individuals had struck enormous on the grounds that they had confidence in the vision of new businesses almost immediately before they exploded. Take a gander at individuals that got tied up with Facebook, Uber, Amazon, Alibaba, Google and numerous others before they turned into the monsters they are today. Today is difficult to realize which organization would explode. In this manner, you can decide to exceed everyone's expectations private venture companies are going. This is anyway not a great fit for everybody as it is restricted to supported financial backers. They for the most part put resources into speculative stock investments, land, and other privately owned businesses. It is useful for long haul financial backers, and you will track down more easy revenue. The danger relies upon the organization you are putting resources into, i.e., on the off chance that it is in organization you are putting resources into, i.e., on the off chance that it is in 15% premium on investments.

7. High-Yield Online Accounts

If you are investigating a generally safe venture, open a FDIC guaranteed high return online record with banks like CIT Bank that proposal up to 2.45% loan fees. You won't bring in a great deal of cash without a moment's delay, yet in the long haul, you will have acquired significantly more than in case you put your cash in a typical savings account. Online banks offer great financing costs as they have relatively little overhead to continue to work. They can pay multiple times the premium most customary banks to pay.

8. Money Market Funds A currency market reserve is ideally suited for fledglings who have no clue about what's truly going on with contributing. You should simply search for a respectable currency market store that offers great returns, and they will do all the thinking for you. They are situated in banks and other speculation organizations. There are a few kinds of common subsidizes called record finances that reflect the market file they are attached to. These supports track a specific record accordingly needn't bother with a ton of the executives on the grounds that the basic list seldom changes. The charges for this asset is low, and the lower turnover implies that the duty will less as well. Lower charges mean more significant yields for the investor.

9. Owning a Real Estate Property

It would be rash to accept that all novices have no the means to make large speculations like land. Claiming a land property and acquiring a rental pay has been done for quite a while and it works. On the off chance that you have an extra room, you can lease it out to a reliable occupant. You can likewise claim an investment property and procure a consistent pay while it continues to increment in esteem. Recollect that your rental pay would be likely to charges, home loans, protection, and functional expenses. The rental pay in urban communities can be low on the grounds that the costs are high regardless of the rental pay being high too. This implies that the danger of claiming investment property in a costly city is higher than possessing one in a less expensive region. Similar applies in regions with weakness even with property protection. You can likewise purchase houses fix them available to be purchased at a greater expense. This is an extraordinary method for bringing in more cash despite the fact that you might should be involved regardless of whether you enlist somebody to take care of you. The return is astonishing, and the danger is moderate contingent upon the area of the property.

10. Annuities

They are presented by insurance agencies where you need to pay a specific sum consistently, and consequently, they deliver you month to month profits. It is in every case better to converse with an expert money official prior to contributing in annuities on the grounds that not every one of them are pretty much as great as they sound. Check out the terms prior to purchasing since some charge a ton and may not be a wise venture. It is OK in case you are searching for a zero-hazard speculation and need to procure a pay for a long time. 11. Pay Off Your Debts

You can be earning a steady passive income, but if all of it is going towards repaying debts and mortgages then, you are not benefitting at all. For contracts, search for organizations that are offering preferable rates over your ebb and flow agents. There are administrations online that assist you with looking at rates for changed home loan moneylenders like LendingTree. In case you are reimbursing a charge card obligation or credit at a financing cost of 12%, the beneficial thing about reimbursing it is that you get a 12% straight return. You may not really have huge amount of cash nearby. Hence, it is smarter to take a gander at two potential methodologies. One is the one we have discussed before on renegotiating the obligation to one that offers a lower financing cost. The subsequent way is to unite two obligations and pay the two together at a lower loan fee. The third way is to enlist for an equilibrium move card that permits you to take care of the obligation inside a predefined period at no extra cost.

Advantages

1. You can pick what works for you. Contingent upon your level of pay, there are numerous venture choices out there for you.

2. Building your speculation portfolio can be a resource over the long haul as you can use it when you really want to. You might even resign in case your aloof ventures bring in sufficient cash for you to live serenely on.

3. It is ideal for individuals who see nothing about the business sectors. The majority of the speculation is frequently made via prepared experts making it ideal for acquiring without overseeing anything. Any reasonable person would agree that despite the fact that another person handles your speculations, you should keep track to check whether you are acquiring or losing.

4. Long term financial backers benefit more from ventures in light of the fact that they procure more profits. Likewise, a few assets additionally give better loan fees for investors.

Disadvantages

1. It isn't by and large the fastest method for bringing in cash. It requires persistence and a sound technique to acquire a decent pay even in the long term.

2. Even however a few speculations guarantee high return, assuming you check out the return you get eventually, you will understand that it was not worth your time in any case. This implies that prior to contributing, an expert would assist you with bettering comprehend the projections before you submit your cash in an endeavor that won't give you exceptional yields eventually.

3. For a fledgling with minimal expenditure and no ability, significant yields might be tricky. The individuals who procure better livelihoods are the people who will chance a great deal and work to improve bargains. Exploration and cooperation might be the best way to acquire a superior income.

4. Investing can be a significant hard theme for individuals who are not into money and financial matters. There are hard terms to comprehend, and the arithmetic can be much really confounding however which isolates somebody who makes an astute venture from one who goes with the breeze is some fundamental type of contributing knowledge.

5. Some individuals overlook retirement accounts as a type of contributing but they are okay and are burdened significantly not exactly other speculation accounts. Great retirement reserves incorporate 401(k)s and Roth IRAs.

6. Most individuals just set aside cash in speculation records and neglect to utilize some of it. It is alright to utilize a portion of the cash you procure on yourself. Try not to delay until you are too old to even think about partaking in the cash that you have buckled down on the grounds that others will.

A Short message from the Author:

Hey, are you enjoying the book? I'd love to hear your thoughts! Many perusers don't have a clue how hard surveys are to dropped by, and the amount they help an author.

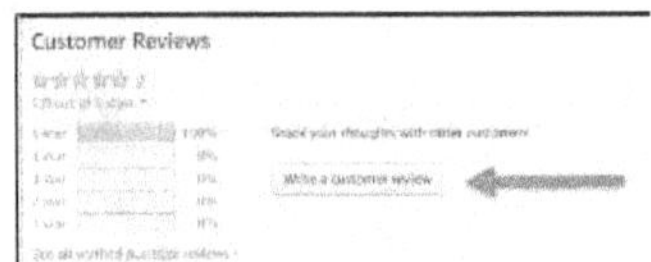

I would be inconceivably thankful if you would require only 60 seconds to compose a short audit on Amazon, regardless of whether it's only a couple sentences!
>> Click here to leave a fast review

https://www.amazon.com/audit/make review?asin=XXXXXXXXX

Thank you for taking the time to share your thoughts! Your survey will truly impact me and assist with acquiring openness for my work.

Chapter 4: Leverage Social Media

"He who makes $25,000 yearly through easy revenue is more advantageous than he who procures $100,000 every year through a salary."

— Mokokoma Mokhonoana

Everyone and their grandma are via online media these days. The chances made by online media as another sort of occupations and organizations have arisen because of web-based media. Individuals across the globe can speak effortlessly these days on account of numerous informal communities out there. There is likewise something for everybody relying upon what you are into. To interface with loved ones, Facebook may be for you. If you want to know what is happening now or trending, then you might be a Twitter person. Those that like to share their everyday lives through brief recordings can think about Snapchat. Instagram is for individuals that esteem photography and excellent feel while Pinterest is the thing that you might need your life to resemble. It presents suggestions on style, design while as yet being useful. For those that need to figure out how to do anything and associate with individuals with comparable interest, think about YouTube. In case you are into informing and sharing amusing images, WhatsApp might be more a good fit for you. These are only a couple of the famous online media destinations out there, and more are coming up each day.

With Facebook having 2 billion, Instagram with 800 million and Twitter with 330 million dynamic clients consistently, it is no big surprise many organizations have quit disregarding web-based media as a spot to advertise their items. Starting at 2017, many huge organizations and SMEs had added more cash to their online media showcasing financial plans. From that point forward, an ever increasing number of organizations have perceived the force of powerhouses is selling their item on friendly media.

How to Find your Niche on Social Media

It's miserable to say that there is the same old thing that you can concoct to draw in a crowd of people via web-based media today. Everybody does likewise things, however they add their character to it. You should simply search for something that you are great at and will seek after it as far as possible and show improvement over some other individual in that specialty. To be a cosmetics craftsman, get familiar with the specialty and accomplish something other than what's expected that individuals have not seen before.

Creativity via web-based media is which isolates the people who make it from the people who don't. It is great to adhere to each specialty in turn via web-based media so you can develop and turn into an expert on that specialty. Be the individual individuals look for when they are searching for new procedures to apply to compensate for instance. Be the one to place individuals on new items on the lookout. This way
individuals trust your perspective and brands perceive your impact over your local area. You can capitalize on this leverage to get compensated to acquaint new items with your audience.

There is additionally such an incredible concept as being too specialty. Individuals get exhausted rapidly assuming they can foresee the following substance. Be flighty yet don't wander excessively far from your specialty. It's additionally great to check out what others in your specialty are doing as such that you can get a reasonable perspective on where your specialty is at. See what is well known and fuse it yet in addition think about the thing is missing and add that to your substance. Examination and check whether your specialty is versatile and influence your crowd to make yourself some money.

After picking a specialty you know, you can be great at, guarantee you pick the right online media stage for you to begin chipping away at. I realize it is enticing to be noticeable on all web-based media stages however it uncommon for somebody to work effectively in case they are giving under 100% on every stage. Probably, pick two of your top choice and work on those. When you have an after, your devotees you follow you any place you are. Pick a stage that suits your specialty. In case it requires visuals think about YouTube, If it requires an internet based store, Facebook and Instagram might do the job.

Case Study: How to Make Money on Instagram

Let 's glance at one web-based media stage and perceive how you can bring in cash from it. Instagram was at first as a stage to share photographs with loved ones, however it has changed to be more expert. Huge and independent companies the same are utilizing the stage to draw in more clients. Certain individuals have had the option to use the business side of Instagram and their supporters to get by off it.

.Leveraging higher numbers

A record with really following and a decent commitment can contact more modest records in a similar specialty and propose to assist them with trip at an expense. It very well might be specifies or a shared post contingent upon the terms concurred, however the more modest channel will get very a few supporters from the bigger record. This will possibly work in case the two records have comparable substance and specialties since supporters will just follow what they are into. There are additionally specialty commitment bunches on Telegram and Instagram's Direct Message that charge a one-time expense to join where little records can associate with more powerful records. They offer commitment helps where individuals in the gathering can work together, bring in cash and associate with each other.

.Sponsored Content
  We have all seen that #ad on a portion of our cherished character's posts.

That implies that they are teaming up with an item to acquaint an item with their crowd. It can either be a video, a notice or a progression of posts relying upon what the individual and the brand settled upon. The individual called an online media force to be reckoned with gets compensated a specific add up to set up that post for them. They might be found in an occasion facilitated by the brand, they might take photographs with the photograph they are promoting, or they might do a full audit of the item. Bigger records can charge an organization continuously the post keeps awake on their page while some might charge per post. The force to be reckoned with charges dependent on the social reach, likely leads and possible clients that purchase from the brand from their after. With Instagram, organizations can either pay for notice on your feed or on Instagram stories. It is critical to sign agreements with the brand you are working with so you guarantee you get compensated for your work. An agreement is likewise significant in light of the fact that it plainly states what is needed of both parties.

.Flipping Instagram Accounts

It is a recognizable cycle where a force to be reckoned with can purchase a little record, develop its followership and sell it at a greater cost. They don't need to do a great deal since they can help commitment from their record. It is as yet a lethargic cycle, however it gives better returns.

.Selling your Products

If you have the numbers and right now know how to advertise on Instagram, the subsequent stage is offering your items to your crowd. You definitely know what they like and have sufficient input to make an item that tackles an issue. You can likewise open an internet based store and begin offering to your supporters which is a way many individuals are bringing in cash on Instagram. Since Instagram is a visual stage, numerous creatives have utilized it to showcase their specialty. Picture takers and videographers are a portion of individuals that have benefitted the most from displaying their work on the stage. Individuals have gotten
lucrative agreements to work with the absolute greatest brands by labeling them on work; the maker figures the brand might like. Applications like Stylinity permit your adherents to buy content from their beloved powerhouses. With each buy that is made, you can procure a commission from alleviating that is sans now on your page.

.

Managing Other People's Instagram Accounts If you have been on Instagram for some time and comprehend its calculation, it very well may be simple for you to turn into an online media chief. You simply need to take the substance which the proprietor of the record sends you and post it at the best time with proper substance. Contingent upon your course of action, you may likewise deal with answering to remarks and direct messages. Online media the executives is an independent ability that is popular today particularly for huge organizations or characters that don't have the opportunity to manage webbased media themselves. A few organizations that deal administrations recruit web-based media administrators to answer people groups questions on the web and deal arrangements. You can likewise be a specialist and proposition exhortation to passional brands on the best systems to develop and associate with their audience.

.Being a Brand Ambassador

This is very like supported posts aside from you are the essence of the brand. You will be needed to go to dispatches and consistently talk about the brand to your crowd. You will likewise have to utilize the brand's item only relying upon what is settled upon by the two players. In return, the powerhouse gets compensated routinely by the organization. Search for exceptional brands a methodology them for a drawn out organization. The most effective way to find a brand minister work is in case you develop your own image and have an objective after that a brand might need to relate with.

.Affiliate Marketing

You can advance items on your page by connecting their connections wilt in the bio space or on Instagram Stories. Individuals are bound to purchase assuming you give a legitimate perspective on the items and it settles a need they have. They will likewise purchase on the off chance that it is in your page's niche.

How to Grow Your Social Media Following

1. Consistency

No matter how great your substance might be, your supporters actually expect you to think of new substance routinely. Assuming it is video content, create a routine to such an extent that your supporters can know when to anticipate new substance. Even social media algorithms favor people that are more consistent and suggest the accounts to more people. 2. Authenticity

The strain to get more devotees causes individuals to do insane things for likes and follows. Individuals will quite often duplicate individuals that are doing great in the expectations that they will get more adherents. Actually individuals are not dumb, and they can isolate who is genuine and who is phony. You might acquire a few supporters that way however keeping them is a genuine test particularly assuming you don't have the foggiest idea what you are doing. Try not to counterfeit it till you make it via online media since it will misfire on you.

3. Link All your Social Media Accounts

People incline toward various web-based media stages, and you can in any case use that with the substance you post. By connecting all your web-based media accounts, you don't have to continue to post similar stuff all around your foundation in light of the fact that there are applications accessible for that at this point. Certain individuals will likewise begin following you in one stage since they saw your substance on another platform.

4. Host Campaigns, Giveaways, and Competitions

The mark of online media is to have some good times, and individuals appreciate accounts that have fascinating things continuing. Assuming you are inventive, you can think of fun rivalries that your adherents can take part in where the victor returns home with something decent. This is additionally a way you can elevate items to your supporters since you get to present the item through giveaways for the victors to give them a shot. Your supporters will impart the contests and missions to their companions and that you will acquire new followers.

5. Interact and Collaborate

The beneficial things about web-based media are that it doesn't separate who the crowd is. You can converse with individuals in your specialty and gain from them how they became their after. You can likewise team up on various tasks on
 each other's pages and procure adherents from each other. Recall that nobody owes you anything and they are not committed to working with you. You can begin by being amicable and supporting their substance online like preferring their photos, sharing it and drawing in with them in the remarks and direct messages. A decent and productive business relationship is the one that is developed through genuine friendship.

6. Hashtags

Since their origin, hashtags have had the option to interface individuals with similar interests and likes. There is a local area for pretty much anything on the web and the most effective way to observe it is through web-based media hashtags. You can add well known hashtags in your substance or essentially the ones that are pertinent to your specialty and individuals who like your substance will remain. In case you are advancing something, you can make your hashtag and urge individuals to bounce on it. No one can say for sure, it might go viral.

7. Use Geotags

The same way hashtags associate individuals with comparable likes and interests, so do geotag with individuals in a similar area. All online media destinations have a method for adding where you are posting on, and others can see it too.

8. Use Insights and Analytics on your Site

Analytics and bits of knowledge are vital for somebody who considers webbased media in a negotiating prudence. It permits the record holder to take a gander at what the crowd likes and what they don't. It additionally tells that person who is keen on their substance, where they are from and surprisingly the best an ideal opportunity to post. Some even applications can even tell which other web-based media destinations new devotees are coming from. With this data, it more straightforward to design your substance to suit the interest, making your page more interesting to individuals and brands.

9. Make More Video Content
 All online media stages are accepting the force of video content. YouTube

acquired a ton of prominence as individuals could identify with content since they could see the individual they like and their character. Other online media stages have added comparative functionalities where the client can add brief recordings. It is additionally accepted that video is the fate of promoting as more and
 more individuals incline toward are getting away from print media and composed work.

10. Paying for Advertisement Social media locales acquire most of their pay through paid notices on their foundation. They likewise offer publicizing or their clients to contact individuals with comparable interests. Paid promoting via online media is somewhat modest considering the measure of contact you get. What's more that doesn't represent the sharing that would follow assuming individuals like your item or content.

 11. Quality Content

They say quality written substance is the final deciding factor and I concur. There is no alternate route with regards to giving quality to your adherents. Assuming you need the ones you need to stay close by, it is smarter to give them the best rather than doing all the other things to add more adherents. Individuals will consistently join in case they see something they like. Regardless of whether you are selling things, do it quietly or join it in what you as of now do as opposed to making your page resemble a bulletin. Individuals consistently notice shifts in your substance particularly those that have been with you for some time.

A disclaimer here is that there are a lot of cons and trick craftsmen that will move toward you and your developing record and guarantee that they can sell you like, supporters and different things however it isn't great. These are bots that have no genuine worth particularly in case you consider your record a business. You want to record commitment and criticism are genuine so Developing your online media pages will set aside time, yet when you have an authentic after, you can make bank.

Chapter 5: Making Money from Websites

To acquire independence from the rat race, one should be either an entrepreneur, a financial backer or both, producing automated revenue, especially on a month to month basis.

Robert Kiyosaki

The web is loaded with sites on various specialties and themes. There are two ways to make money from domains: One, buy a new domain, and then sell it and two, buy an expired domain, then sell it. Both of these techniques can be called space flipping. There is likewise one more way where one buys the areas, chips away at the site and develops it and later sell it at a more exorbitant cost with content and traffic. That is called site flipping. Area flipping is moderately less expensive on the grounds that you should to develop naturally so the

you can use that later on. simply purchase a decent space name that can be sold later at a greater cost. With site flipping, one invests a ton of energy and assets raising it from the beginning, and the profits are a lot higher than area flipping. There are those individuals that will purchase sites to flip and that can be hazardous on the grounds that it may not be as rewarding particularly for a fledgling. Area flipping is more straightforward on the grounds that one needs to distinguish great lapsed space names, get them and keep them till a decent arrangement goes along. Space flipping is quicker in light of the fact that there isn't a ton of subtleties to it; each of the one requirements is an interest in the area name, and the arrangement can be settled. The equivalent can't be said about sites on the grounds that there is a ton to consider before somebody makes the buy. As a novice, you can begin with area flipping and get familiar with everything on what is rewarding, and what isn't. You can likewise realize what to do assuming you ultimately choose to begin flipping sites. You will realize where you can trade sites in light of involvement and know-how.

What Makes a Domain Name Lucrative?

For an amateur, the principle question will be, how might I let know if an area name is productive or not? There are sure components that you want to see while choosing worthwhile area names:

How long is the domain name? As I said before, the internet has a lot of websites, and most of the short domain names are taken as of now. Thusly, assuming you get an area name with 3-4 letters, it is important on the grounds that it's impossible you will see one that isn't now taken. These area names are important on the grounds that they can be an accurate match to the name of a brand or a company.

How old is it? The older the domain name (one registered over ten years ago), the more likely to have a lot of backlinks. Backlinks are a sign a website has authority. Therefore, both age and authority can determine the price of a domain name.

Can it make a brand? When looking at short domain name with random letter combinations, look at it critically to see if it can be used in branding. Some are more straightforward than others.

Is the domain extension on the domain name valuable? The domain name can have 3-4 letters and may seem perfect but look at its extension. Look for domains with popular extensions such as
.com, .gov, .edu, .net, .org etc. There are uncommon extensions that can still work so don't rule anything out.

Are the words in the domain name searched on search engines? You should consider taking domains that have a high search volume on popular search engines such as google.com. That means that the domain will be on demand.

Does the domain name contain a popular term? Many businesses and brands are coming up every day so you should choose a name that could be of interest. You need to discern because a business may not exist now, but the domain name could still be valuable. Even if the domain name is highly searched, it should also have low competition among the searches to ensure uniqueness. Look at all these aspects on a keyword planner to make the right choice.

Is the domain name the name of a person? You never know if a person may be interested in a domain name of their name to create a personal brand.

There are two methods for deciding whether an area name is adequately significant to purchase: Buying spaces dependent on famous points or in light of how select they are. Point based areas are rewarding on the grounds that they can contain the name of a famous specialty, business or brand that would be not difficult to flip. Select domain names are rewarding on the grounds that they are stand-out and can never be enlisted again. Normal words and 3-4 letter combos are restrictive as they were enlisted at the origin of the internet.

How to Start Domain Flipping

1. Find lapsed area names

The web has numerous space name commercial centers where one can look and purchase terminated space names. Space names lapse when its proprietor neglects to recharge it with the area enlistment center. The space enlistment center is the specialist organization that enrolled the area name in any case. At the point when the space name isn't enrolled, the area recorder offers an elegance period, typically 30 days where the proprietor can in any case pay and hold their space. Assuming no installment is made in the time specified, the space recorder records the area in a public sale. The purchaser needs to check for the accompanying prior to purchasing the lapsed domain:

.Domain Authority (DA)

This is a SEO metric that allots a worth between 1-100 that shows how high on an internet searcher the site would rank. Number 1 is the most elevated score while 100 is the least. Moz.com concocted this decimal standard by checking out the count of backlinks to the webpage, its social sign, the nature of the substance in the site the Moz Rank and Trust and how effectively the web search tool crawler can move in the site. DA takes a gander at the entire website.

.Page Authority (PA)
 Here, the page is the focal point of the evaluation. .The Quality and Count of Backlinks/ SEO Profile

The older a domain, the more the backlinks it will have. Even if it has a lot of backlinks, they should also be of good quality, i.e. they should be legitimate. A poor-quality backlink is full of spam from suspicious referring websites and too many backlinks coming from suspicious niche websites from using services from Private Blog Networks (PBN) and not organic backlinking from good quality websites. There are research tools that can help you do extensive backlink research such as Ahrefs or moz.com.

.The History of the Domain of the Expired Website.

Investigate in case there were different proprietors of the space name before the past proprietor. Some 3-4 letter space names might have been utilized for different things prior to arriving on the closeout. Along these lines, it's smarter to investigate prior to purchasing a space name with things. Use archive.com to affirm its protected to buy.

.Bans on Google

Check on the off chance that AdSense or Google prohibited your space name prior to purchasing, if not you probably won't get a purchaser for it. Use isbanned.com to see whether it was prohibited from google the web index and bannedcheck.com to preclude a restriction from Google AdSense.

2. Buy Expired Domain Names

There are numerous sites online that offer space barters. Recall that some of them might expect you to pay a month to month charge to partake. A few sites incorporate DomCop, ExpiredDomains, Domain Hunter Gatherer, Domainhole.com, Godaddy.com, Dropcatch.com, JustDropped.com among others. You can likewise set aside some cash when purchasing terminated area names by utilizing promotion codes utilizing Groupon.com.

3. Sell your Domain Name

There are a couple of commercial centers that you can sell your space names, for instance, Bido.com, Flippa, Namepros.com or Sedo.com. Assuming you have assembled a space flipping specialty site, you should offer to your email list subscribers.

4. Set a Price for your Domain Name

As we had examined before, the cost of every area name relies upon numerous different elements, in addition to the purchasing cost. In the event that it popular, assuming it is selective or on the other hand if it brandable; every one of these are factors that can be utilized to set the cost of your space. You can likewise pay attention to the value the potential purchaser is offering and afterward arrange. With time, you will actually want to tell the price tag every area lies relying upon the market. The cost of spaces varies from that of sites. The worth of a site is in the rush hour gridlock it gets in a predetermined period, its substance, current and likely income and the SEO profile of the
 site. If all else fails counsel an organization that can run an investigation and provide you with the gauge of the website.

5. Use Expired Domain Names for your Own Website Some individuals search for lapsed space names for something beyond

flipping. You can purchase a definitive area name and start your blog with it. Certain individuals purchase terminated area names and use them for their backlink potential. You can do this utilizing 301 divert which connects the area name to your site when somebody taps on it. A portion of the old area names are better compared to enrolling new space names. Utilizing stopping specialist organizations, you can acquire from commercials on the area name site particularly assuming it gets traffic from blunders and reference traffic sources. Utilizing terminated area name sites, you can construct your own PBN by guiding them to your site. In any case, you must be mindful so as not to seem like your site is being spammed which can cause more damage than great in the long run.

How to Start Website Flipping

1. Pick a Niche that you will Focus on.

The specialty of your site ought to be founded on your enthusiasm and information. You can likewise pick a well known specialty that individuals are looking for on the web. The specialty ought to be evergreen to such an extent that individuals will consistently be searching for it online for quite a while to come. This guarantees you continue to acquire an easy revenue for a long time.

2. Choose Main Keywords

Use a free or premium Keyword Planner to decide the watchwords that you should use in your site for SEO purposes. It ought to likewise have low rivalry (under 100000) so it can bear outing from different sites in the equivalent niche.

3. Add Supporting Keywords

From the principle watchword, you will require another 15 catchphrases or more that are pretty much identified with the fundamental catchphrase so you can compose content based
on them. The more the articles, the better you will acquire in the future.

4. Buy a Domain Name with your Keywords

If your domain name matches the keywords you have selected, then your website with rank high on google searches. You can either do this first and work in reverse or trust that you get something in the specialty you have picked. Either way, a good domain name coupled with a good extension such as .com or .net will rank quicker on search engines.

5. Write Content for the Website

Pick a format that takes into account AdSense and starts chipping away at content. You ought to have 50-70 500-word articles distributed on your site. Utilize your catchphrases no less than multiple times; in the title, in the first and last sections and in the body. Utilize one watchword for every article.

6. Submit your Website Online

Don 't simply post your site and trust that the internet searcher crawlers track down your work. This might consume a large chunk of the day in light of the fact that your site is still new. Present your work directly to the accommodation sites of all the well known web indexes you know.

7. Market your Website Online

Now you really want traffic prompting your site. You want to observe individuals that are searching for your specialty through online media sites and different sites. You can likewise attempt visitor presenting on power destinations on get backlinks to your site. Attempt however much you can to procure quality backlinks to help your website.

8. Earn Through AdSense.
Apply for AdSense and guarantee that your site is positioning on the top page of all inquiry engines.
9. Put it on Sale

There are sites that you can list your site marked down like Sitepoint.com. In case your site is positioning on the top page and has good
quality substance, then, at that point, you are headed to making the deal. Add the automated revenue that it is now producing then you will have hit the jackpot.

Chapter 6: eBook Publishing

You become monetarily free when your easy revenue expenses.
 T. Harv Eker

Writing a Book

Writing an eBook is difficult, and it most certainly responsibility. You require a month forward to compose a book beginning to end. As a matter of first importance, you need to consider what you are energetic about. As I said, composing isn't quite so natural as many individuals make it appear. It is considerably harder to expound on a point you don't know anything about. Think about your experience, abilities, information on a specific theme and expertise.

You should designate opportunity to would your examination on what you like to compose and check whether there is a business opportunity for it.
surpasses your

requires some Search for watchwords that are famous in the class you need to expound on and make an idea you figure individuals would be keen on. For verifiable, think about what is well known, however for true to life, there is a wide scope of classes to look over on independently publishing destinations. The mystery here is to know when to put it up.

The following stage is to search for an intriguing and appealing title that suits your subject and is not difficult to recall. This is more significant for fiction since it's what individuals will recall your book as. True to life is more tolerant on the grounds that you just need to remember the well known catchphrase for the title. Utilize your title to let the crowd know what they will get from your book. Incorporate the time span to make it really captivating, similar to How to Earn $1000 a Week Selling eBooks in 2019.

If you have all that, then it's time to plan what you are going to write. I demand, quality written substance makes all the difference and ought to be what is important most in your book. Regardless of whether you settle on a long or short book, you should enhance the peruser with your substance. Now, it is great to think about taking a web based composing course in case you are not a certain essayist. Have a blueprint of what your book is concerning that you can follow until you complete the book. Recollect that you can add
and take away what you need from the layout as you compose the book.

After composing the book, you should peruse and fix some plot openings, particularly in fiction. You can get some beta perusers that can assist you with your story. When you are certain that your story is OK, continue on to language structure. Utilize any language structure actually looking at instruments and fix normal mix-ups. You can go above and beyond and enlist an expert proofreader to take care of you. Presently it's an ideal opportunity to begin with the distributing process.

Self-Publishing an eBook

Many individuals are tricked to accept that independently publishing their own specific manner is a reason not to buckle down. All things considered, it's simply posting it on one of the numerous independently publishing locales and that it. Wrong! You should prepare yourself for the long and horrifying work in front of you with the goal that you are totally ready. Nonetheless, this isn't to debilitate anybody not to seek after this choice to distribute their book. Independently publishing is the main choice for man individuals in light of the fact that there are not many customary distributers that are taking risks on new, unpracticed composes these days. Since the choice of doing it without anyone else's help is accessible, why not attempt it. If you are determined and willing to put in the work, then, this is the process for you.

1. Format your Document into an eBook Readable Format When you are composing, you will likely utilize a word handling record and

organization utilizing something very similar. This is OK if it somehow managed to be perused utilizing a similar word record, however since it isn't, the arranging should be unique. You need your book to be discernible by any eBook peruser accessible in the market since perusers will not have the one you use. There is no compelling reason to utilize headers, footers or page numbers in an eBook. This is on the grounds that the peruser isn't enthusiastic about page numbers and the eBook peruser will add its own headers and footers. Your headings ought to have heading styles so the peruser will recognize themes and subtopics. Your passages ought to be designed utilizing the primary line space to make the peruser stream flawlessly starting with one section then onto the next. Make sure to isolate one part from another utilizing page breaks. The equivalent should be possible for segments. Your pictures ought to be of the.jpg configuration, and they ought not be wrapped. You can add them to the focus as inline pictures. There ought to be a singular page that shows your title and caption and one more discrete on showing copyright guidelines. The ISBN number can either be shown on the cover sheet or the copyright page. The following page should show your book's Table of Contents to illuminate the peruser what's in store in the book. The utilization of heading styles makes producing a chapter by chapter guide exceptionally simple. Your cover page/picture ought to be the main page of the book.

2. Make an eBook Cover that Suits your Book and is Attractive to the Reader

I 'm certain you have heard the axiom don't pass judgment prematurely. Indeed, they weren't right in this example on the grounds that many individuals will pass judgment on your work by the cover you present them. The more appealing the cover is, the almost certain individuals will buy your book. In this progression, guarantee that you take some opportunity and arrive up with something everybody will love.

There are two methods for getting an eBook cover for your book. The first is most likely the least demanding, i.e., recruit an expert to do it. There are endless independent locales where you can get a specialist to accomplish the work for you at a reasonable rate. They even think of numerous examples for you to pick the one you like the most. The second ay might be tedious however assuming you are imaginative can be enjoyable.

To make your eBook cover, recall that you will require a picture of 1659px by 2500px, the size of the width and length separately. A few locales might request a more modest picture; in this manner it's dependent upon you to do your exploration. Try not to put a line around the picture. Utilize the standard RBG (red, blue and green) shading file for your picture. Add the title of the book and the writer's name in a text style everybody can peruse. Try not to utilize an excessive amount of calligraphy with the goal that everybody can comprehend. Stay away from pixelating the picture and avoid profane images.

3. Convert your Document to eBook Readable Format

The re are many conversion software's out there that allows you to convert your book to acceptable formats such as .epub, .mobi, and .pdf. The .pdf design is very simple on the grounds that most word processors permit you to send out your report in this organization. Regardless of whether they, there are a lot of programming on the web that can even do that free of charge. The .mobi design is accessible to the
Caliber word processor. You are not needed to do The transformation yourself as the product will do it for you albeit in certain cases the outcomes may not be as you would prefer. This configuration is simply satisfactory to Amazon and Amazon will change over it into .epub design. The .epub design is somewhat more complicated than the other two. You can adhere to directions online on the most proficient method to change over to from .doc to .epub arrangements, or you can take the simpler course and search online for transformation software.

4. Check your Cover Before Uploading it Anywhere

Once you have changed over your book into the .epub design, you will in any case have to check whether it looks great. You can download the organized picture and utilize an eBook peruser to open the archive and see it is up to standard. The significant spots that ought to be of interest are the cover picture, the chapter by chapter list, the pictures in the book, projectiles, and numbering and all pages of the book ought to be in the arranged book.
5. Do Some Final Touch-ups assuming your Book Needs it.

In case you found some mistakes, there is software such as Sigil that you can use to make your changes. Assuming that the book is adequate in your guidelines, you can distribute on one of the accompanying sites.

.

Amazon

.

Kindle, Apple

.

on iTunes

.

Barnes &
 Noble, Ingram

.

Scribd

.

Google
 Play

.

or Baker and Taylor

A Step by Step Guide to Marketing an eBook

Months before the launch

There is no particular opportunity to begin advancing your book. The prior you start, the better, regardless of whether you just had the thought. This is on the grounds that you can include your perusers in the process so they anticipate the day you dispatch the book to them. You can likewise get some input en route to further develop your creative cycle. The most effective way to do this is through an online media stage. Observe the locales your perusers could be on and when are they on the web. You can likewise verify what they like to peruse. You ought to have a Facebook record and one on Goodreads. Start on marking as quickly as time permits to make a local area of individuals that will back you up. Get individuals to join to your email list. This ought to happen roughly 2-3 months. Assuming you have something to show your crowd, do as such as of now like passages, book cover or day for kickoff. Get them amped up for the book.

A month to the launch

Have persuasive individuals talk about your impending book or day for kickoff. In the event that you are done, this is an ideal opportunity to begin sending free examples to certain individuals. Allow them seven days to peruse and circle back to questions. You can request that a few bloggers survey your book and remember to express gratitude toward them. Request that they rate your book on Amazon so your book positions at the top when it is dispatched. On locales like Goodreads, Amazon, Publish Drive's foundation makes your book accessible for preorder and set a day for kickoff. Pick a less aggressive class or two for your book. Use YouTube to show a book trailer which is a pattern with the present scholars.

One week to the launch

You are nearly toward the end, and this is the place where the showcasing ought to get more exceptional. Begin utilizing your email list by sending them tokens of your dispatch. Get cautious via online media and get individuals to begin discussing your book. Contingent upon your assets you can give an official statement or simply pay individuals to create a buzz around your dispatch. Now, it is smarter to begin collecting a dispatch group to help you upon the arrival of the launch.

The Launch

The most ideal way to make the most deals from your book is by sticking to search for the best an ideal opportunity to set up your book. Consider the accompanying schedule for various genres.

.January
 Good types to distribute are; inspiration, wellness, motivation, self improvement and objective setting.
 Bad Genres to distribute are; mid year books, fiction.

.

February
 Good types to distribute are; verse, love, and heartfelt books.

 Bad Genres to distribute are; plans and whatever other fiction that isn't centered around adoration and romance.
 .March
 Good sorts to distribute are; baseball and most games classifications, ladies centered books.
 Bad Genres to distribute are; Travel and self improvement books. .April
 Good types to distribute are; Easter and other strict books, and fiction, life stories, and diaries, books on WWII.
 Bad Genres to distribute are; Winter and occasion books, fiction on affection and romance.
 .May
 Good types to distribute are; Parenting books, Fiction, history, and summerbased books.
 Bad Genres to distribute are; Fiction on affection and sentiment, self improvement books.
 .June

Good types to distribute are; Books on nurturing particularly parenthood, contemporary fiction.
 Bad Genres to distribute are; Fitness and sentiment fiction.

.

July and August
 Good types to distribute are; Any substantial understanding books, fiction. Awful Genres to distribute are; Self-help books, occasion books.

.September
 Good kinds to distribute are; Books on journals, governmental issues, history, school, and school (Educational reads.)
 Bad Genres to distribute are; Fiction, particularly love and romance. .October
 Good classifications to distribute are; Dark verifiable particularly secrets, thrill rides, and horror.
 Bad Genres to distribute are; Fiction, particularly love, sentiment and fantasy relationships.

.

November Good types to distribute are; Children's books, occasion books, formula, and cookbooks, strict books.

 Bad Genres to distribute are; Fiction particularly love and sentiment, self improvement books.
 .Decembe
 r

Good sorts to distribute are; Don 't set up
 anything. Terrible Genres to distribute are; Most
 books.

Remember to have some good times, converse with individuals and associate. Answer questions individuals might have on your book consistently during that day.

One week after the launch

It's an ideal opportunity to show appreciation to individuals who worked with you before the dispatch, during the dispatch and after. In the event that at this point you have begun getting reviews,
 make sure to say thanks to them as well. Since you have a book search for ways of promoting it on the web. Scan the web for programs that will assist you with advertising to more people.

One month after the launch

Your deals won't be on a vertical development, and the time has come to begin offering deals and limited arrangements to keep individuals intrigued. The book will partake in a spike in deals, however from that point forward, it's better to allow your organization to do the advertising for you. This will possibly occur assuming that your book is good.

Chapter 7: Renting Your Belongings

Make cash, don't allow the cash to make you. Change the game; don't let the game change you.
 Macklemore

Most of us have such a large number of things that we don 't utilize simply lying around. There is a market out there for leasing things we presently don't utilize however are as yet in working condition. This might be befuddling in light of the fact that a great many people don't have a clue where to begin with regards to making automated revenue with the things they currently own. Others are frightened on the grounds that there are numerous unpalatable characters on the web that can be risky. This isn't to imply that you can't get great individuals to pay you for utilizing your stuff. We will perceive how you can lease your stuff to make extra money.

What would you be able to Rent Out to Make Some Money?

1. Rent Out Your Wedding Gown

It is silly how much a wedding dress expenses particularly on the grounds that you can just wear it once. That is the explanation certain individuals decide to bring in some cash by allowing one more lady to have it for their big day. A few sites permit you to add an image of the dress and when it endorses, you will actually want to procure some automated revenue from your dress. A model is Borrowing Magnolia that even aides you boat, clean, and keep up with your wedding dress.

2. Rent your Living Space

Some individuals have enormous homes or extra rooms that can be utilized by vacationers and guests at an expense. What is the point of searching for occupants when there are locales like Airbnb, Wimdu, HomeAway, and VBRO (get-away rental by proprietor) that interfaces a vacationer to a delightful home that they can remain in while they are visiting a spot. Don't worry about damages because Airbnb covers you with close to a million dollars. They just take a little commission, and you get to keep the remainder of the cash. You can make game plans with the tenant on the most proficient method to get the keys and store. Some even have the choice of picking the occupants they need in their home. There are locales like Giggster that permits you
 to list our home or part of your home as the expected arrangement of a film or TV series. How cool is that!

3. Rent your Car

Some individuals have vehicles, however they don 't utilize them regularly. Others have numerous vehicles and store them in the carport when they can lease it out to bring in cash. You can enroll with Turo and Getaround lease your vehicle to individuals in your neighborhood procure a level of the benefit. You can decide to lease it until your vehicle arrives at a specific mileage and the hour's kin can lease your vehicle. For wellbeing reasons, you are the one in particular that can give the tenant a code that opens the entryways. Installments are made month to month, and they fuel your vehicle upon return. You can likewise employ your vehicle to drivers for organizations like Uber, Lyft and Hyrecar and procure more pay. These applications are offer taxi administrations on individuals' vehicles. The vehicle is guaranteed and safe on the grounds that the organizations track them. Assuming you have a RV away, there is additionally a business opportunity for that through RVshare that permits you to lease your manufactured home at a charge. Same goes for motorbikes through Spinlister.

4. Rent your Parking Spot

If you live in a populated area or a place that experiences a lot of traffic due to events, then you might want to consider renting your parking space for some extra cash. Sites such as JustPark or ParkingSpotter can help you get a renter for your parking space. There is the choice of making it a long-or transient arrangement, contingent upon what you are agreeable with.

5. Rent your Storage Space or Garage

Some individuals have a carport with a ton of room that they can lease to individuals with a ton of things they seldom use. Assuming you have space and can get somebody able to lease your carport, you should simply get a tenant contract, and both of you sign it, and afterward you get to procure automated revenue month to month. StoreAtMyHouse and Craigslist can assist you with finding leaseholders for your space at a commission and free individually. A similar applies to an extra room that you may not be utilizing that another person needs.

6. Rent your Clothes

If you have a stunning feeling of design and style, then, at that point, this one is for you. If
 you have a ton of popular outfits that you don't get to wear regularly, you can consider StyleLend that permits individuals on the site to wear your pieces of clothing. They offer protection against harm or misfortune. Guarantee everything is all together prior to sending it out to the middle. You can value your thing from 5-10% of the things market esteem. They give you 80 % of the cash they get.

7. Allow Campers on your Land at a Fee

Some destinations that permit you to lease a home likewise permit campers to lease setting up camp stuff from the proprietor. In the event that you additionally have sufficient land to fit a campground envision the measure of cash you can make from both. In any case, Gamping interfaces campers to landowners who need to lease setting up camp space. Campers can either bring their stuff or you as a leaseholder can give everything to them to make more money.

8. Rent your Tools

Whether you have the big tools that cost a lot of money or simple household tools like screw gun, hot glue gun, vacuum cleaner, etc., FatLAma, Zilok, T'work, PeerRenters, and Loanables are there for you to list the tools you are not using to get renters. You can rent per hour or per day that's up to you. The bigger the equipment, the more money you shall get for it. Get yourself some insurance to protect yourself against liabilities in case of injuries. Talk to the renters and ensure you get a higher deposit in case of damages. You can also rent out everyday equipment like drones, musical instruments or cameras to professionals that need them. You can use Toolsity for that.

9. Rent your Boat

People who live close to huge water bodies generally have boats. The boats might be fishing boats or houseboats where individuals can put in two or three days at the marina. Destinations like GetMyBoat and BoatSetter interfaces individuals who are searching for a boat with boat owners.

10. Rent your Baby's Old Gear
 Baby stuff can be costly, and since your kid has as of now grown out of a

large portion of the extravagant stuff you got, you can think about leasing it out to unseasoned parents. Use BabyQuip to associate you to unseasoned parents who might require these things for their baby.

11. Rent an Event Space

If you have a yard adequately large to fit an enormous gathering of individuals, you can consider leasing it out on destinations like ThisOpenSpace, Splacer or PeerSpace. You can indicate the time that the occasions can be held in your space. Depending on the size of your space, events like birthdays, team building, wedding photoshoots, baby showers, anniversary dinners and so on can be held at your space at a fee.

12. Rent out Yourself

Yes, you heard me. Yourself. It's anything but a grammatical mistake. Individuals can do nearly anything on the web and, for this situation, assist them with observing a companion in the nearby area that they can spend time with or converse with. They can likewise lease companions in various regions of the planet with the goal that they have organization when they are in an unfamiliar region. RantAFriend.com permits individuals to observe individuals they like to interface with as companions. You can offer your administrations as a companion who might incorporate; talking, walling them around time giving private visits, offering guidance, going out to parties, watching films and feasting out. You can charge by exercises or number of hours, that is dependent upon you. There is a site called BridesmaidsforHire that permits ladies to employ individuals to be at their wedding party.

How to Earn Money Doing Stuff you Already do

There are huge loads of stuff we accomplish with the expectation of complimentary that we ought to be paid for. A portion of these exercises occupy the majority within recent memory at any rate, and it is an alleviation to realize that we can get compensated to do them. This is an exceptionally appealing deal particularly for individuals that are in school and need the additional cash. There are many organizations out there that expect individuals to assist them with understanding the market or are simply searching for criticism on their items and will pay for these administrations. A portion of the things that you as of now do and ought to be paid for include:

.Getting your Money Back for Online Shopping

For those that are into web based shopping, incalculable money back programs permit you to get a good deal when you burn through cash on their sites. Since you as of now shop on the web, this is a decent method for bringing in back a portion of that cash you have as of now spent. One would think about how they can give you cash back when you shop. You see, when you shop through a certain website's portal, the sellers pay a commission to said websites, They then give you a percentage of the commission because you shopped through their portal as customer appreciation. The same applies to some credit cards such as Discover it that offer cashback rewards to its customers.

.Earning Through Surfing the Internet

We are always on the internet searching for answers, looking for things and even connecting with friends. What better method for bringing in some additional cash by utilizing a web crawler to peruse the web and getting a commission webpage like Qmee, Swagbucks and Inbox Dollars offer cash to its clients for utilizing their pursuit engines.

.Earning Through Watching TV

Some apps allow you to watch an array of videos online and then reward you with points that you can redeem for many things including money. A few sites pay you to marathon watch shows, and you get an allowance while others pay you to watch and offer your fair perspective in return for cash. Models incorporate Watch Netflix, Perk. Television, National Consumer Panel, Nielsen TV appraisals, Nielsen Digital Voice, Success Bux, etc.

.Save Money by Booking Hotels and Flights on Travel Websites

Even however you in fact don't bring in cash through this strategy, it is assisting you with keeping the cash you as of now have. For individuals that affection going via air, you can consider utilizing on the web venture out destinations to book your movement and convenience to save some money.

.Earning Money Through Grocery Shopping

Many individuals know the cash saving specialty of couponing is the main way you can set aside cash when looking for their food. Furthermore, a few locales permit you to search for refund items to such an extent that when you are shopping and end up purchasing such an item, you can check your receipt and get your cash back. They likewise offer money back remunerations for their clients. A model is Ibotta.

.

Earning Money for Keeping Fit
 There is a portable application focussed on health and wellness where you can join and finish specific wellness undertakings for you to do. You vow to do these undertakings inside a determines period, and you get cash in your record. You will, notwithstanding, be fined on the off chance that you neglect to get done with the responsibility. This isn't an issue for somebody that is committed to wellness and working out.

Chapter 8: Making Passive Income as An Artist/Creative

If you don 't figure out how to bring in cash while you rest, you will work until you die.

Warren Buffett

The explanation I decided to place specialists in a different gathering is that there is an excessive amount of shame confronting the workmanship business. By craftsmanship, I don't really mean drawing or painting however any work of art that individuals figure one can't make a profession out of. As far as I might be concerned, craftsmen are those that make and sell candles, underground artists, assuming you make shoes, guitars, jam, stew thus some more. They utilize their minds to make things that we want on an everyday premise. They might not have sufficient cash to promote, yet they actually need to get by from their thoughts. This part is intended for anybody that utilizes their creative mind to make anything.

How to Earn a Living as An Artist or Creative

1. Stock Photography

Some people don't know that you can sell your photographs online to people. They assume that you can only get money by getting clients to pay for your skills. There are many people out there that take photos of buildings, plants, animals or landscapes that are not paid by someone to do so. They enjoy the work and would like to know how they can make more money from their photos. There are websites online that buy photographs from talented photographers. Depending on the site, the photographer can be offered a commission every time someone pays to use the photo, or the website can the photo. If camera and don't know what to do with them, you can create a portfolio and approach one of these websites, e.g., Shutterstock. Other sites include Alamy, Picfair, EyeEm, Foap, iStockphoto, Dreamstime, Free digital photo Getty Images, etc. Even if you get a commission from the website, you have no control over what the
just give the photographer a one-time fee, and they now own

you have those beautiful pictures f your phone or DSLR

individual who commission is installments insofar as individuals utilize your work. How might you have your work endorsed by one of these websites?
 is authorized by the site does with it. Paying you a the more ideal arrangement as you will get online

.

Have a theme for each photo you take and choose the best from each theme. They only need the best shot; otherwise they could reject your work because of duplication. Keep your submission to 10 photos.

.

Some websites have millions of photographs, and they have different categories for each one of them. It is already hard to get in one of these websites, but it is even harder if you submit a photo in a popular category. Do something unique that they may not have seen before, and you are guaranteed to be accepted. Keep your best materials for later and start with a simple yet beautiful shot.

.

Avoid submitting photos that capture brand names or trademarked items. That would cause your photo to be rejected for copyright infringement. Avoid people's faces, public places or commercial objects. You may submit them in the future if you're accepted.

.

Keep your images the recommended size. Ensure that they are visible and meet the standards of the website you are submitting to.

.

Edit your photo before submitting. Many software allows you to do so. You can remove vignettes, add color among other things. Never submit photos with lens flares.

2. Licensing your specialty to third parties

Here, you need to search for individuals who need your craft say a photo, music, application and offer them a permit to utilize your item for your work. You will bring in more cash this way as you are the one that will set a cost for what you think your work is worth. You should have an interesting item and search for individuals that you think can purchase a permit for it. There are numerous ways of doing that, i.e., through online media, email records and conveying proposition. Don't simply trust that individuals will coincidentally find your work. You can
 market your work anyplace on the web where you can contact more individuals quicker. You get to bring in cash authorizing the item every time they restore the permit while you actually get to keep your product.

3. eBooks We have discussed independently publishing and selling eBooks before in this book; thusly I will avoid through this. Despite the fact that I ought to advise you that the book ought to be founded on the thing you are doing. You can do a presentation of what you so and afterward be innovative with your substance. You can make a guidance guide or some other data you might need to impart to your reader.

4. Start a Blog Related to your Art

Any business out there is needed to have a site nowadays, so should you for your specialty. For individuals to treat you in a serious way, they need to see your portfolio or test of what you can do before they are persuaded to purchase. Having a blog also allows you to apply other passive income generating avenues such as advertising, affiliate marketing, email marketing and selling your art online. You can likewise make a participation site that you can impart to your paying crowd unique work and your interaction. You make a month to month pay instead of making them purchase something only a single time. You will need to accomplish more work of making new items to keep the individuals fulfilled, and you will require more refined programming to keep up with your site to oversee installments and usability by clients. Regardless of the responsibility, you will procure more this way than the wide range of various methods.

5. Make Money by Selling Social Media Shout-outs to other Smaller Artists

If you have a decent after via web-based media, you can bring in cash by moving toward more modest gifted specialists and inquire as to whether they would pay for a whoop. Some will concur, and some might not have the cash to pay you so it's dependent upon you in case you can assist somebody gifted by utilizing your foundation for great. It is vital to recall that you ought to just be giving yell outs to individuals in your specialty. You would rather not confound your crowd by presenting an alternate specialty in your space except if it's a coordinated effort that is tied in some way to your niche.

6. Be a Part of an Artist Collective

It is in every case better to impart thoughts to individual craftsmen than going with regards to it alone. The vast majority want to attempt to create it on their own when it very well may be simpler collectively. Imaginativeness, for instance, is one of those ventures that wouldn't work as expected assuming individuals neglected to convey and motivate one another. Instead of battling as a destitute craftsman, interface up with different specialists that can assist you with selling your item or workmanship. With individuals doing comparative things or even various things however in the creative business, you can think of cool tasks you can do together. You can begin craftsmanship displays, and you can make specialty gatherings or clubs. You and a gathering of your comparative disapproved of companions can search for ways you can help the local area you live in through youth projects, instructing classes to the penniless and assist with moving more individuals to join the arts.

How to Make an Online Course and Make Money Selling It

The explanation I have excluded this subject of making and selling your own web-based course as a method for making an automated revenue as a craftsman is that it is the principle way for a craftsman to bring in cash. The main thing a craftsman truly has is the ability and what better method for utilizing that ability than to bundle it and sell it on the web. Various stages permit a craftsman to do that however before then how about we take a gander at how to make an online course.

1. Find a Subject Matter

You previously recognized the ability that you have and need to impart to the world. Its opportunity to take a gander at it inside and out and check whether you have sufficient material to fit a whole course. You should accompany some fascinating materials that individuals would be keen on paying you for. Make a title that incorporates the center abilities your course will confer on your understudies. In your depiction advertisement a few more center abilities that you guarantee they will leave with after they complete your course. These are what will empower you to design your illustrations, make advertising simpler and convey your point across to your students.

2. Find Out assuming that there is a Need

This is significant since, in such a case that individuals are not intrigued by the subject you need to instruct, then, at that point, there is no compelling reason to do it by any means. This is the place where you can check out what
 individuals are saying on the web and track down what else you can remember for your course. You really want to begin diving more deeply into our course so you are not gotten ignorant when questions begin coming in.

3. Make a Teaching Plan and Course Outline

You need to consider your time and when you are free for the illustrations. Converse with your local area on the web and ask them when they are allowed to take your course and plan around that. You then have to think of how to structure your lessons. Are they in modules or weeks? What should each module contain and how can I make it as interactive as possible? How long are each module and the course in general? Make sure you cover all the bases before you dive in.

4. Consider your Teaching Methods.

Each student is different, and you might want to cater to their different learning styles. Some learn from looking at pictures while others like working on the lessons through a quiz at the end. You can look for feedback to find the best delivery method like text, video, guides, audio, worksheets, etc. You can combine two methods to teach your course.

5. Make your Content

This s where the greater part of your work will be. You need to guarantee that you convey something valuable to individuals who will take your course; any other way, you will get a tone of terrible surveys. You likewise need to make the responsibility simple for them to follow and pose inquiries when they don't. The recordings and sound ought to be clear for everybody to follow what you are saying. Brand your material appealingly so that individuals know what they are taking. After you finish the work, go through it again and ensure it is sufficient for the understudies. Before you get arrogant and imagine that you have made the best course ever, it's memorable's critical that all that you have composed can be tracked down free on the web. Bundling your work in an advantageous, straightforward way is the thing that makes individuals intrigued by your course. They need to know everything identified with your center abilities without talking with other sources.

Here is the means by which to sell your course online:
1. Plan How to Sell the Course
Assuming you as of now have a site, add the highlights that you should
convey the course to your local area. Assuming you don't, start with that.
There are different modules particularly on WordPress that assist you with
the selling and conveyance of an internet based course. In case you are not
talented in making such a site, you can sell your seminar on different sites that generally offer that help like Skillshare or Udemy. You will, nonetheless, need to impart to the site a piece of your income relying upon the business you make. The benefits of these sites are that you don't need to stress over conveyance frameworks as they deal with selling the course and handling installments. You should decrease the expense of your course in light of the fact that the opposition can get extremely steep. You additionally don't control your work since you are not running the course. There is a superior choice that consolidates two of the distinctive conveyance styles. You gain to influence what the substance resembles yet keep up with the advantages of a web-based course site. Instances of such sites incorporate Ruzuku and Teachable.

2. Upload your Course Online

Depending on the stage you decide to convey your course, you should tweak your course to look interesting to the understudies. You should utilize noticeable text styles, an alluring shading plan and your logo for marking purposes. Individuals should have the option to perceive your brand.

3. Marketing

As with all the other things in this book, individuals need to know what you are doing before they come ready. You should utilize different web-based media locales, blog, email list and numerous different roads to explain to individuals why they need to take your course. Online media has paid compensation per-click publicizing choices that you can pay for to contact more individuals in your specialty. It likewise permits you to see who is keen on our page among different bits of knowledge that can assist you with assembling a showcasing plan that suits everybody on your local area. In your showcasing pitches, center more around what the understudies will escape the course rather than zeroing in on selling the actual course. You can let them know what's in store in case they take the course. In case you have different courses, offer them tributes that can be checked so they can trust you. You really want to advertise your work locally in light of the fact that they as of now trust you. Offering to outsiders is harder
 on the grounds that they don't have any acquaintance with you and can't prove assuming you are certifiable or not.

4. Update your Course Often

Things change consistently as is the thing that is in your course. You really want to do visit examination to work on your substance, adding what you figure individuals might need to know and eliminating what is as of now out of date. Continue to go through the connections in your course to check whether they are as yet working. No one can say with any certainty assuming the site you were alluding to eliminate the substance or quit existing out and out. These little subtleties are which isolates you from awful reviews.

5. Collect Feedback
 If you are a veritable vender, you will need to circle back to your

understudies to check whether they got anything from your work. Assuming they had any issues, it's vital to know so you can address them later on. Take their encounters so you can utilize them for your tributes in the future.

6. You can Create more Content Through the Steps Outlined Above

Advantages of Passive Income for Artists

1. People get to perceive your work in light of the web-based stage. Gone are the days that specialists expected to truly show their work. You even have a more noteworthy crowd through showcasing yourself online rather than actual spaces. This implies you can make more money.

2. You get to gain from others in a similar field. Individuals doing likewise get to meet one another and talk about their techniques for procuring automated revenue from their art.

3. You get to venture to the far corners of the planet and still make more workmanship regardless of where you are. You can speak with individuals you are showing on the web which is consistently an or more. Nobody cares where you are the length of you convey your item to your subscribers.

The end… almost!

Reviews are not easy to come by. As a free writer with a little advertising spending plan, I depend on perusers, similar to you, to leave a short survey on Amazon.
Even assuming it's simply a sentence or two!

we 've learned en route up to this point. In the prior pieces of the book, you were informed on the significance of fostering a tycoon mentality and for what reason that is significant in turning out to be monetarily free. Likewise, you were presented to the numerous issues and difficulties that individuals face with respect to their accounts. We additionally discussed the vital initial steps that you really want to take with the end goal for you to get this show on the road towards accomplishing monetary freedom.
 Now, you should be presented to the a wide range of factors and factors that may decide your achievement in your endeavors.

The explanation that you must know about these variables is that these ideas can really help the way that you decide to structure your life. To lay it out plainly, you can provide your activities with a superior feeling of direction in the event that you realize what sort of effect they can have on your objectives. For instance, one of the fundamental factors that we will address today is the advancement of one's mental ability. If you know that getting smarter is going to lead towards success, then you can structure your daily habits around trying to fuel your knowledge and increase your intellectual capacity. Consciousness of these elements and factors can just assistance you in laying out your objectives and your activity plans for yourself.

In this section, you will be presented to three significant factors specifically. To start with, there is mental ability. As a business visionary and thought pioneer, you are restricted by what your psyche can fathom. So, if you have a limited intellectual capacity, then it's going to be very difficult for you to develop certain skill sets that can give you a competitive edge. Then, there is the element of one's social abilities. Clearly, it is basically impossible for you to have the option to do everything all alone. You should have the option to take advantage of the assets that are made accessible to you by individuals who encompass you. Finally, we are additionally going to discuss the significance of keeping up with uprightness and unwavering quality with the way that you work.

Intellectual Capacity

Why is it that Bill Gates finds it so important to hire smart people for his business? Is there really any truth to the idea that kids who get high grades in school are the ones who end up becoming more successful in the future? How smart do you have to be in order for you to achieve your goals? These are
 a portion of the inquiries that we will attempt to reply in the underlying piece of this section. Doors himself conceded that his strategy for recruiting is fairly elitist. Yet, is that a terrible thing?

A Case for High IQ

Actually, there is some examination that proposes that more astute individuals will generally make for better laborers. In light of boundaries set by Psychology Today, IQ envelops different parts of intellectual capacity, in particular, critical thinking, language securing, and spatial control. A standard IQ test would include these perspectives. Commonly, somebody with a score of 100 on an IQ test would be viewed as normal. Analyzers who score over 125 fall under the top 5%.

According to an article distributed by the Harvard Business Review, there are three spaces of execution in which workers are assessed: capacity, social abilities, and drive (Chamorro-Prezumic, Adler, and Kaiser, 2017). The writers of the article pressure that with regards to deciding a representative's latent capacity, organizations need to measure how logical it is that an individual would have the option to acquire or dominate complex abilities. Furthermore the most effective way to measure one's latent capacity is through IQ or intellectual ability.

One of the most famous asset materials that present a defense for employing individuals with high IQ levels is a paper that was distributed in the Journal of Personality and Social Psychology back in 2004. The examination was initiated by Frank L. Schmidt and John Hunter. Basically, what their examination found is that more intelligent individuals will quite often perform better in the work environment since they were better and quicker at learning new skills.

Increasing Your IQ

Don 't stress In case you don't have an IQ score that falls inside the scope of the tip top. Like some other ability throughout everyday life, your mental ability is something that you can practice and expand on extra time. With the end goal for you to be really fruitful, you want to put a ton of time in yourself. This implies you putting forth a deliberate attempt to hone your psyche and sharpen your abilities. The further you put resources into yourself, the better you will become at dealing with every day issues and difficulties that any business visionary or expert may confront. In request for you to truly develop your mental ability, attempt to follow these tips:

1. Work on your creative mind. Recall that any sort of achievement just emerges from envisioned outcomes, openings, and potential outcomes. If you force yourself to be more imaginative with the way that you think, then you are essentially expanding the realms of possibility for you to succeed. With a solid creative mind, it will be simpler for you to tackle issues, grow organizations, and fabricate solid associations with individuals you work with.

2. Put yourself outside of your usual range of familiarity. However much you might not have any desire to hear this, genuine development and advancement happen outside of one's usual range of familiarity. This is expanding your viewpoints. If you only stick to environments and projects that you're already familiar or comfortable with, then you are stymying your own growth. You ought to consistently allow yourself an opportunity to acquire another viewpoint by drenching yourself in circumstances that you've never been in before.

3. Never be without a book. If you survey all of the people in the world who are generally deemed successful, it's likely that all of them have a habit of reading books. Cutting a couple of moments or hours out of your day to participate in perusing can truly help grow your perspective and hone your acumen. At the point when you read, you are basically captivating in an uneven discussion with the writer. Any book that you read, regardless of whether positive or negative, is continually going to uncover to you something that you won't ever know. On the off chance that you're not a major devotee of perusing, book recordings can help too.

4. Try your hand at entertaining riddles and tests. Get a sudoku or a crossword puzzle from time to time. Download applications on your telephone that are intended to hone your intellectual capacity. Play memory games or speed-thinking works out. Partake in critical thinking exercises. These encounters assist with building the neuroplasticity of your cerebrum. This implies that your cerebrum will improve at shaping neural associations. Thus, it can work at more elevated levels. Like some other muscle in your body, in the event that you reliably practice your cerebrum, it gets stronger.

5. Make learning a propensity. This is a point that will be elaborated upon further in a later part. But in a nutshell, you should always consider yourself as a student. You ought to try constantly to gain from others or from solid source materials. When you are constantly feeding your brain with new information, then you are also widening your knowledge base.

6. Exercise routinely. You probably won't feel that running on a treadmill can make you more intelligent, however it truly does. At the point when you have a strong and predictable exercise routine set up, you are basically working on your body's capacity to ingest oxygen. Also your cerebrum really works better when it is loaded with oxygen. Henceforth, actual exercise can likewise assist with reinforcing the cerebrum. A portion of the advantages that accompany having a cerebrum that is loaded with oxygen incorporate further developed memory, center, and intellectual function.

7. Practice great resting propensities. Not getting sufficient rest can significantly disable your intellectual capacity. Subsequently, you put a limiter on yourself at whatever point you're simply barely getting by. Getting sufficient rest and recuperation while you rest is crucial for preparing your brain for a day loaded with learning and intellectual activity.

Social Skills

We 've as of Presently covered how having a high IQ can assist you with tracking down progress. You've additionally been shown how you can expand on your mental ability consistently. Now, it's an ideal opportunity to address one more significant driving element to progress: EQ. You may contend that social abilities are getting less and less significant in a work environment where everything is by all accounts moving towards mechanization and advanced correspondence. Notwithstanding, the opposite is in reality evident. In a paper by David Deming named"The Growing Importance of Social Skills in the Labor Market," the most lucrative positions, which are hard to mechanize, require a high dominance of social abilities (2017).

The explanation that social abilities are turning out to be increasingly more significant in the present work market is that PCs are as yet unequipped for precisely reproducing genial human collaboration. Not at all like positions that require incredible arrangements of numerical and scientific abilities, businesses and organizations need to depend on human resourcefulness for occupations that have a substantial social viewpoint to it. Indeed, it can be simple to get a PC to do the math and run some examination. Notwithstanding, a PC doesn't have the range of abilities that is important to settle a negotiation, to broaden an association proposition, or to relate to a client. Likewise, the main part of usefulness which is profoundly affected by friendly abilities is group collaboration and science. No fruitful organization is worked by an independent person. Generally incredible organizations and brands of the world are made by groups of devoted specialists and workers. Considering that, the usefulness of most organizations is reliant upon how its laborers work as a solitary unit. What's more the way where they cooperate is intensely directed by their social skills.

So, with the goal for you to truly embrace a tycoon outlook, it's insufficient that you transform yourself into the most intelligent individual in the room. You actually should know how to play with others. When you are convicted and passionate about your ideas, then that's a good thing. You can contribute extraordinarily to rejuvenating that thought. Notwithstanding, when you can energize a group of troops behind you to assist you with emerging your thought, your capability to succeed is colossally amplified. Considering that, something beyond chipping away at your smarts and your keenness to assist you with climbing to the next level, you additionally need to deal with your social abilities. Here are a portion of the abilities that you should work on:

Positivity and Optimism

While it would be reckless to make a speculation, there is motivation to accept that most specialists will more often than not respond emphatically to positive energy. Even something as simple as smiling at another person can instantly uplift that person's perception of you. An immense piece of having the option to work with someone else adequately is setting up a feeling of trust and brotherhood among you. Normally, you can accomplish that assuming you permit yourselves to become OK with one another. To this end it's critical to proliferate a climate of inspiration with individuals you work with. It's simpler for you to get individuals on your side assuming that they don't fear you.

Empathy

Empathy is basically one 's capacity to have the option to identify with the sentiments or musings of another person. Setting aside the effort to truly tune in and sympathize with someone else will permit you to comprehend them more. And when you gain a better understanding of what makes a person tick, then you will be able to figure out how to get the most out of their potential as well. It additionally becomes simpler for you to work with individuals with whom you share a common arrangement and regard. Toward the day's end, there is a ton to be acquired from understanding individuals you work with. The individual with a mogul mentality realizes that compassion is one of the main devices that they need in their toolbox.

Cooperation

Again, you can indeed do a limited amount much all alone. Your capacity to play with others is truly the thing will take you over the top. As somebody with aspiration and drive to succeed, you should have the option to figure out how to help out others. This means you can work successfully with others to deliver yield that could never be conceivable in case you were working alone. There is strength in numbers. What's more the more individuals you can get to assist you with satisfying your objectives and dreams, the more straightforward it will be for you to succeed.

Listening

One fundamental rule that a great deal of pioneers will more often than not disregard or dismissal is the specialty of tuning in. Again and again, aggressive and driven people will be so OK with giving orders and establishing the rhythm. Obviously, these are significant qualities to have at whatever point one is attempting to move to progress. Nonetheless, these should never come to the detriment of figuring out how to pay attention to other people. All things considered, the main way you can truly expand the capability of individuals that you work with is for you to get what really matters to them. Individuals with mogul outlooks comprehend that it takes a town to raise an organization. So, if you want to be in the business of success, then you must also be in the business of people management.

Assertion Without Aggression

As you advance on your excursion towards progress, you must force a many individuals to share the vision that you have. To do this adequately, you should be outfitted with the ability of statement without turning to animosity. It tends to be so natural to become forceful in attempting to influence individuals to see things according to your perspective. Nonetheless, the vast majority don't ordinarily react well to hostility. In fact, it's likely that aggression will end up being detrimental to your pursuits for collaboration and teamwork. You should have the option to sort out some way to be more decisive with regards to your bearing and your techniques without depending on hostility. Furthermore this is most certainly a craftsmanship more than science.

Open Mindedness

Lastly, you truly need to rehearse the ability of receptiveness. Once more, since you have solid feelings concerning where you need to go and what you need to do doesn't consequently imply that you're correct. You want to free yourself up to periodic analysis and input. By being receptive, you are adequately permitting others to be a second, third, or fourth arrangement of eyes. You may be caught unaware by your own sentiments and feelings concerning seeking after your objectives. It's critical to have individuals around you who have you covered and draw things out into the open when you're missing something.

Integrity and Reliability

It 's not an embellishment to say that honesty is a significant quality that can assist you with improving your life in a comprehensive way. To speak the truth about it, honesty is really one of the center mainstays of somebody with a tycoon mentality. When you look at a person who has a successful and happy life, it's very much likely that you are looking at a person with integrity. At the point when you have respectability, it basically implies that you maintain truth and genuineness with each part of your life. And if you continue to stay honest with yourself and everyone around you, then you are effectively ensuring your own personal success.

 Make no slip-up with regards to it. Uprightness is something that you can chip away at. Like an individual's insight and sympathy, you can generally hone your trustworthiness throughout everyday life. Recall that the propensities that you practice consistently at last create your person as an individual. And if you practice the habit of maintaining your integrity in whatever situation you find yourself in, then you're going to turn out all right. You may not understand it, however having respectability can really assist with upgrading different qualities and rules that you have in your life. This is on the grounds that trustworthiness instructs and urges you to consistently remain consistent with what your identity is. At the point when you are an individual of honesty, you never feel it important to change what your identity is quite selfishly. Regardless of how extreme life may get, you generally adhere to your standards and your convictions. Furthermore when you carry on with an existence of uprightness, it's so natural for you to simply be straightforward with yourself. This, thusly, makes you more dependable and reliable according to other people.

On the unpleasant street towards progress, it tends to be exceptionally enticing to pursue faster routes at whatever point the chances to do as such introduce themselves. It very well may be so natural to simply quit any pretense of doing the entirety of the difficult work and hop directly to the end goal. Notwithstanding, individuals with uprightness comprehend that throughout everyday life, there is no such thing as alternate ways to progress. Fostering a tycoon attitude implies understanding that it's more with regards to the excursion and the cycle than it is about the reward.

An individual with trustworthiness isn 't really worried about the oddity that accompanies being fruitful. If someone is too focused on the perks and the quirks that come with success, then that person is missing the point. Achievement in itself can't be accomplished when the attitude and the strategy are completely wrecked up.
 What you get when you cheat and exploit others to get what you need is just the deception of progress. That sort of "achievement" is brief and impractical. At the point when you carry on with an existence of honesty, this is the thing that it truly means:

You Never Compromise on the Importance of the Process

Having respectability implies realizing that you need to confide all the while. It doesn't make any difference what life might toss your direction; you won't ever move on your standards and your convictions. In case you realize that there is a way for you to swindle your direction to the top, you won't ever do as such. You comprehend that going against
 your standards just to get what you need won't ever be inside the domains of possibility.

You Do the Right Thing Because It's the Right Thing to Do

When you have uprightness, you don 't simply make the best decision on the grounds that others are watching. It's likewise not simply making the best decision since it ends up helping you also. Assuming that were the situation, what is to prevent you from doing some unacceptable thing when no other person is watching? What is to prevent you from accomplishing something horrendous when you realize that it will help you anyway?
 People with respectability comprehend that there is an inborn virtue to anything that they do. Also this worth is undaunted by witnesses, results, or expectations.

You Keep Your Promises

An individual with uprightness is continually going to remain consistent with their guarantees. Recollect the multiple occasions in your day to day existence wherein individuals have missed the mark on the guarantees that they gave you. Did your impression of these individuals change after these occurrences? Clearly, when you are anticipating that someone should convey and they wind up missing the mark, you grow a feeling of doubt towards that individual. That is the reason an individual with trustworthiness never makes guarantees that they have no goals of keeping.

Obviously, there will be times wherein you can not follow through on a guarantee since you just couldn't do as such. It's not on the grounds that there was an absence of exertion. In those occasions, maybe your inadequacies can be pardoned. In any case, generally, an individual with uprightness won't ever energetically make a guarantee that they will not keep.

You Face the Truth

When you have trustworthiness, you don't avoid reality. You don't flee from it. Whether or not it's a badly designed truth or not, an individual with trustworthiness will never really conceal it. To be fruitful, you must have the disposition that is needed to confront the cruel realities. At the point when you are checking out deals insights or client surveys, you aren't continually going to like what you see. What's more when you won't acknowledge reality, then, at that point, you are viably actuating your own demise.

Also, individuals with honesty won't ever be occupied with beguiling or deceiving others. As has been recently settled, you generally need the up front investment of individuals around you to track down accomplishment throughout everyday life. What's more there are not many manners by which you can distance individuals around you more than by being underhanded. When people realize that you're being untrue and dishonest, then you become unreliable in their eyes. You will lose their up front investment and you will wind up battling your battle on your own.

Integrity is a Mindset - A Millionaire Mindset

Integrity, in itself, is likewise an outlook. It's something that you should completely epitomize profoundly. Trustworthiness is something that you really want to completely embrace and coordinate into each fiber of your being. It's not simply something that you practice at whatever point it's simple or helpful. Respectability isn't only some arbitrary thoughtful gesture, trustworthiness, or liberality. Respectability is a lifestyle. In particular, it's the lifestyle of the effective. If you want to be able to develop a millionaire mindset for yourself, then you must embody the principle of integrity in your life.

Benefits of Drop Shipping

Drop transporting is a quickly developing industry due to its many advantages. The following are a couple examples:

1. Less Capital

As expressed in the main part, outsourcing organizations don 't have to deal with and store stock for their business. Consequently, an outsourcing business doesn't need colossal measures of capital. This is the greatest benefit of this sort of plan of action since it doesn't need the surge of cash just to purchase inventory.

Traditionally, entrepreneurs expected to burn through a large number of dollars on stock before kicking off their business. With outsourcing, these entrepreneurs can place their cash into something different beside stock, similar to the advancement of an expert website.

2. Purchase upon making a sale

With outsourcing, vendors just need to buy stock at whatever point they make a deal to their clients. This implies that an entrepreneur doesn't need to go through his own cash to purchase stock. It is really conceivable to begin this business with very little cash in light of the fact that the clients will actually be the ones paying for the stock from the suppliers.

3. Easy to Start

Anyone can begin an outsourcing organization from the solace of their home. Beside the tiny measure of cash expected to begin an outsourcing business, this plan of action is not difficult to begin. You should simply observe a solid provider with an extraordinary item that can be offered to the market. The key here is to know who to work with and what items to sell.

4. Low Business Risk

With an outsourcing organization, there is an altogether lower business hazard. Since you don't have to burn through a large number of dollars in stock, you won't be left with a ton of unsold stock on the off chance that the business doesn't succeed.

Have you at any point watched the Pursuit of Happiness? Will Smith 's perIn this wayn was exceptionally hopeful with regards to his new undertaking. Notwithstanding, since his item was not sought after in the clinical business, he experienced difficulty selling it. Likewise, he purchased the whole stock in advance. So, when he was unable to sell his products, he ran out of cash which might have been utilized for different basics. With outsourcing, you won't need to stress over getting into a comparative situation.

5. Low Overhead

Aside from low capital prerequisite, you will presently don 't have to spend much on overhead since you won't have to oversee heaps of stock. Indeed, countless outsourcing organizations are really overseen by proprietors through their homes, basically with the utilization of a PC. Drop transporters that work from home wind up going through gencrally $100 every month on overhead.

Obviously, the measure of overhead will ultimately develop as your organization develops, yet this is moderately lower contrasted with other blocks and concrete or conventional business models.

6. Wide Array of Products

When it comes to what you need to sell in your outsourcing business, the anything is possible. You can actually sell a wide variety of products because you do not have to pre-purchase all of them for resale. However long your provider has a specific thing in stock, you can list that up in your stock for your clients. One might say, you are simply going to be an incredibly viable go-between for the supplier.

7. Flexible Area Location

You can begin your own outsourcing organization anyplace you need, as long as you have a web association. You can even set up your PC close to your bed and begin working without slipping out of your night robe. However long you observe solid providers and you can speak with clients effectively, you can effectively deal with this kind of business.

8. Easy Work Scale

With outsourcing, entrepreneurs can undoubtedly scale their responsibility in light of the fact that the outsourcing providers will do a large portion of the utilizing. You will just have to take in client orders, and providers will bear every one of the extra cycles expected to satisfy that specific request. Subsequently, you can really extend your business with very little gradual work.
 However, you should accomplish client support work, such as managing client questions, yet remember that this sort of issue can be stayed away from in case you by and by know your providers just as the nature of items that they provide.

These are a couple of the most widely recognized motivations behind why this kind of plan of action is developing. These advantages make outsourcing exceptionally appealing to financial specialists. In any case, this doesn't imply that outsourcing doesn't accompany a cost. In the following section, we will take a gander at the inconveniences of drop shipping.

Steps To Creating The Perfect Instagram Name

The Instagram handle that you select should be basic. If you have a business website or domain name, then make sure that your Instagram handle is similar to the domain name. It makes it very simple for others to perceive your Instagram profile. The username should not be dubious or dark. Assuming that is the situation, it will be hard for others to perceive your image on Instagram. Before you begin conceptualizing for the ideal username, set aside some effort to find out pretty much that large number of brands and organizations that fizzled at becoming on Instagram even before they started. Business and brands ordinarily block their development on Instagram when their crowd (target and nontarget) are confounded and don't have the foggiest idea what the brand rely on, distinguish an absence of cohesiveness all through the brand informing and content. Basically, they understand that the username or profile name doesn't match the substance posted on the account.

So, take as much time as necessary and don't be in a hurry while choosing your Instagram handle. It is a good thought to do some exploration and counsel others when conceptualizing thoughts for your Instagram account. You can ask your relatives, companions, partners or any other person to help you en route. Pick a name that suits your image's goals, but on the other hand is in a state of harmony with the advertising methodology of your image. Indeed, you can direct a speedy study to get whether or not the Instagram handle you like is the ideal decision. How about you inform a couple of individuals concerning the likely handles and see their first response? The underlying reaction is frequently normal. If they react favorably to it, then maybe you actually have a good Instagram handle in hand.

If you want to use Instagram as a promotional tool, then it is absolutely vital that your Instagram bio is attractive and inviting. Your profile is the thing that will constrain guests to associate with your image on Instagram. Maybe, one of the fundamental parts of the bio is your image's username. All things considered, this is the principal thing that your crowd will see on your Instagram profile. You should begin considering thoughts that will make it more straightforward for others to observe your Instagram profile. Additionally, you should guarantee that the Instagram handle of your image passes on your image's message. The name you pick will rely upon the sort of crowd you wish to target. It becomes simpler to stand out for your audience when the Instagram handle is novel. To expand your commitment rate on Instagram, a decent beginning stage is get imaginative with your Instagram handle. In this segment, you will be given a few hints that you can follow for making the ideal Instagram username.

Think About Your Hobbies

A decent Instagram handle as a rule enlightens the guest something regarding the brand other than its name. This proves to be useful, particularly assuming your image is related with any type of leisure activity. By doing this, you're making it simpler for your crowd to connect themselves with your image. It likewise builds the odds of obtaining more supporters. For example, how about we expect that you are a splendid gourmet specialist named Danielle. There will undoubtedly be a few group named Danielle on the planet, so you really want to think of an Instagram moniker that will separate you from the rest. Don't simply ponder showing your standard name, rather consider manners by which you can straightforwardly connect it with what's going on with your page. If your Instagram page consists of posts about recipes, the food you cook, and so on, then the username must convey the same. Possibly you can take a stab at something as per @crazychefdanielle, or @danisdeliciousfood. You can get as inventive as you need with the username.

A Name Generator Tool

You can without a doubt lounge around and conceptualize until you get an ideal thought. In any case, this isn't in every case simple, and it tends to be somewhat tedious. Additionally, you probably won't concoct a smart thought night-time of conceptualizing. Fortunately there are different webbased name creating apparatuses that you can use to get everything rolling. Regardless of whether you get a little thought by utilizing these apparatuses, it will give you some force. There are different online username devices like The Cool Name Generator, Spinxo, Screenname Generator, or even Rum and Monkey. Truth be told, a speedy Google search will assist you with this. Regardless of whether you like any of the ideas given by these instruments, you will absolutely get a few thoughts en route. A large portion of these internet based instruments expect you to enter several catchphrases alongside explicit individual attributes for creating distinctive usernames. When you make a rundown of every single reasonable choice, the choice interaction becomes easier.

Use Your Name

You can make an exceptional Instagram handle by joining various words. Now and again, having a remarkable name may work in support of yourself. You can mess with your name and think of a novel handle. You can have a go at joining your first name and your last name and use it as your Instagram handle. It might work, yet invest some energy and take a stab at modifying the letters in your name to shape a one of a kind handle. For example, the renowned tennis player Serena Williams dispatched her own dress line Aneres. Aneres sounds very outlandish and welcoming. The name of the attire line is simply Serena spelled in reverse. You can accomplish something like this too.

Think About Your Audience

When you're pondering your Instagram handle, contemplate the crowd your image obliges. Make a name that will give your crowd a thought regarding what your image rely on. By doing this, it likewise empowers you to stand apart
from the remainder of your opposition and builds the pace of commitment. Moreover, it becomes more straightforward for your crowd to track down you. Invest some energy and examination moving catchphrases or hashtags identified with your image industry. You can utilize the Instagram search element to do likewise. While choosing specific catchphrases, remember that they are not being utilized by your rivals. You can pick watchwords that are related with the items or administrations your image offers.

Unique Characters

You don't need to limit yourself just to the letters of the letter set and can likewise incorporate different characters or numbers into the handle. There are various symbols which you can use like @, #, $, * and so on. In any case, don't get carried away with these extraordinary characters. Recall that the handle should be not difficult to track down and recollect. Assuming the handle is a muddled blend of different characters in letters alongside numbers, you simply make it hard for your crowd to track down you. You can likewise utilize characters for making arises which can be put in your Instagram handle. Even a common name can be jazzed up with a couple of unique characters.

Location

If you have a local business, then it is a good idea to include your location in the handle. Your potential clients may be keen on searching for a particular item or a help in the given region. By adding your area to the Instagram handle, you're making it simpler for your expected clients to recognize your business or brand. It doesn't imply that you basically remember the name of the city for the username. Now and again, it may even check out to incorporate the name of the nation or even the state. For example, the renowned attire brand Forever21 has distinctive Instagram represents every one of the nations it is available in. By doing this, Forever21 is making it simpler for its clients to observe the Instagram handle that is applicable to them.

Using A Title

If you have a professional title, then you can try adding it to your Instagram profile. Adding a title can unquestionably assist with recognizing your image from others. Have you ever known about Dr. Phil, Dr. John, or Dr. Dre? What is the one thing that this large number of individuals share for all intents and purpose? They all have a title added to the name.
 Regardless of whether or not they are genuine specialists, the title makes a difference. If you are a professional, then try adding your title to the Instagram account. It makes the username appear to be more recognized as well as appears to have a pleasant ring to it. Try not to utilize an expert title assuming you don't have one and don't attempt to fool your devotees into accepting that you're somebody you are not.

Competitor's Profiles

Coming up with the ideal username will without a doubt take some time and exertion. However, if you feel like you hit a roadblock or need a little bit of inspiration, then start checking out the Instagram profiles of your competitors. Make a rundown of the relative multitude of individuals who are well known in your industry or specialty and really take a look at their profiles. A fast hunt on Instagram should assist you with doing this. You can't take your rival's profiles, however it will without a doubt give you a thought or some inspiration to concoct an alternate name for your own profile. Basically it will furnish you with a beginning point.

Duplication Of Names

While making an Instagram handle, a typical issue that a great deal of clients run over is that subsequent to observing the ideal name, they understand that it's as of now taken. Given that there are billions of people in this world, it is quite likely that In this waymeone else might have had the same idea as you. In the event that you think of an apparently amazing Instagram name troublemaker, and it's as of now taken, don't stress over duplication of names. At any rate, Instagram won't permit two clients to have the equivalent username. So, the time has come to get somewhat innovative and adjust the username with the end goal that it's anything but an ideal imitation of an existing username. Allow us to expect that the username you need to select is @clarklewis, yet you understand that it is now taken. Presently, you can take a stab at adding two or three unique characters to the fundamental username to make it unique. For example, you can attempt, @clarklewi$ or @clark.lewis.

Using Adjectives

Another imaginative method for making a decent handle is to add a couple of descriptive words. Perhaps you can settle on a particular trait, which impeccably depicts your image. For instance, if you are an Instagram blogger who offers relationship advice to women, then @sassysasha Along these linesunds better than @Sasha. So, take some opportunity and arrive up with two or three descriptive words, which depict and loan character to your image. When you have a rundown of descriptors, concoct innovative methods of adding to them to your Instagram username.

Additional Tips

The Instagram handle you pick should be not difficult to articulate. An individual should have the option to rehash it without recording it. It should be straightforward and should not be equivocal. Assuming any piece of the name is confounding or is obscure, it will only damage your scope on Instagram. Remember that if your username is very like a current username, it can prompt copyright encroachment issues. Along these lines, be cautious while you're attempting to copy another username. Anything excessively near a current username well prompts pointless lawful trouble.

Another thing that you should remember is that the username should not be extended. Whether or not it's a profile for a brand or an individual profile, it should be short and explicit. Adding a word like
 supercalifragilisticexpialidocious to your Instagram handle is certainly not a smart thought. Assuming the name isn't not difficult to articulate, how might anybody recall it? Likewise, a short name offers a specific level of exclusivity.

Avoid utilizing any names that are identified with a particular sex, nationality, religion, or sex. Assuming the name appears to be one-sided, by and by, it will just land you in boiling water. The username should not affront or be one-sided toward anybody. Likewise, don't make the handle excessively normal or nonexclusive. You can surely join a typical word with an extraordinary word to concoct something energizing and engaging, however don't attempt to make a conventional name your Instagram handle.

Initially, it may appear to be somewhat interesting to think of the ideal handle. The principal thing that you should do is quit worrying over it. By following these tips, you can without a doubt comeup with a one of a kind and innovative username.